OPEN FIELD

OPEN FIELD

30 Contemporary Canadian Poets

~

EDITED AND WITH AN INTRODUCTION BY

SINA QUEYRAS

FOREWORD BY

MOLLY PEACOCK

A Karen and Michael Braziller Book

PERSEA BOOKS / NEW YORK

Thanks the poets who contributed to this anthology and the presses whopublish Canadian poetry. Thanks to my students who read, responded to, and were inspired by much of this work. Thanks to Mairead Byrne, Laura Huzzy, KO Kanne, Martin Mitchell, Ron Smith, Gina Wise, Rachel Zolf for their assistance. Thanks to Persea Books, particularly Rita Lascaro (for her design work) and Gabe Fried (for everything else). To the many poets considered, but not included in this anthology, I thank you for your work, and hope for volume two. To Danielle, family, and friends, thank you for your patience.

—Sina Queyras

Since this page cannot legibly accommodate all copyright notices, pages 247–249 constitute an extension of the copyright page.

Requests for permission to reprint or make copies, and for any other information, should be addressed to

Persea Books, Inc.
853 Broadway
New York, NY 10003

Library of Congress Cataloging-in-Publication Data
Open field : 30 contemporary Canadian poets / edited and with an introduction by Sina Queyras ; foreword by Molly Peacock.—1st ed.
p.   cm.
"A Karen and Michael Braziller book."
|Includes bibliographical references.
ISBN 0-89255-314-6 (original trade pbk. : alk. paper)
1. Canadian poetry—21st century. 2. Canadian poetry—20th century.
3. Canada—Poetry. I. Queyras, Sina, 1963-
PR9195.72.O64 2005
811'.54080971—dc22   2005001710
Designed by Rita Lascaro

FIRST EDITION

Contents

Foreword

In 1991, I started commuting between New York City (hub, I thought, of the poetry universe) and London, Ontario. On one trip I stopped in Toronto, ventured into a bookstore, and flipped into a parallel universe. There was a poetry section, but I recognized almost no names on the shelves. It was as if I'd walked into a bookstore in Dublin or Sydney—places far off, not a one-hour flight from LaGuardia. What was going on? Surely Canada, the polite annex of American movies, TV, and ice cream, was an annex of American poetry, too.

Though I was born in neighboring Buffalo and had even been a high school exchange student in Toronto, my awareness of the differences between Canada and the United States was just beginning. It wasn't the border crossing or the picture of the Queen on postage stamps that made me fully understand that I had come to another country. It was Canada's poets, many of whom are in this anthology. In that store, I started writing down all the titles I didn't know, aiming to stuff my suitcases full. As I did so, I noticed that almost every volume had an imprint indicating support from a government sponsored arts council. Was it possible that the Canadian government was actually interested in poetry? (I'll return to this in a moment.)

One morning soon after, I read an essay in the *Globe and Mail*, Canada's national newspaper—an installment of a series of well-crafted personal essays by ordinary citizens prominently featured in the paper every day. *Every day*, I thought? There are enough ordinary citizens who can write this well for a newspaper to publish an essay *daily*? While reading the essay, I heard callers to the Canadian

Broadcasting Company's morning radio show casually discussing Philip Larkin. Whew! Ordinary people talking about poets confirmed this parallel universe as literate, sharp, thoughtful, and educated.

Soon I learned to say "North American"—not just "American"—and "the States," an acknowledgment of the distinct countries on this continent. I discovered poets Daphne Marlatt and Susan Goyette. I acquired *The New Oxford Book of Canadian Verse in English*, edited by Margaret Atwood, and read her well-known observations about the extremities of weather and geography that underpin Canadian poetry. Was a covering of snow the reason why all these poets seemed to be kept some sort of national secret? Or was it the presumption below the border that the Great North was just another candidate for the 51st state? Again, I noticed that Canada Council logo on the books of poetry I was reading. There it was on Sonnet L'Abbe's book, and Ken Babstock's. Why was public money channeled so directly into poetry?

Next, I witnessed a parliamentary election. It was announced suddenly, and the media didn't have time to profile the personalities because reporters were rushing to outline the issues. It was policy, not political personalities, that people were invested in. When I tuned in for the election results on a local TV station, a reporter made a casual reference to Catholic schools getting government money. I felt an almost biological frisson. No separation of church and state! Monarchs on the money! Parliamentary government! Poets I'd never heard of! Finally, it dawned on me. Canadians (including the poets) were living out the consequences of huge historical movements. I was not in a place that had been settled by Puritans. I was not in a place with a myth of rugged individualism or a policy of manifest destiny or a 200-year-old Declaration of Independence. I was not in a place that had fought and won a Revolutionary War.

Imagine Canada and the U.S. as two wary sisters in the 200-year aftermath of a family crisis. Think of English-speaking Canada as the daughter who stayed attached to the parent, while the rebel child cut ties. Think of the notions of filial responsibility this engenders, the attachments to civility, to the lowered voice, to the effort to negotiate, to work things out. Think of all the peace-keeping roles Canada plays throughout the world and of how long it took Canada to come into its own. Canada's constitution is not yet 40 years old.

Think also of the country's bilingual dynamic. Language defines culture, and here, I distinctly heard two. Not only was there a whole set of Anglophone poets whose work I didn't know, but also a whole body of poetry in French. Around the time of the election, I discovered Erin Mouré, a translator of French-Canadian poetry, who writes her own poems in English.

The American idea of the melting pot does not exist in Canada. There is no ethos or mythology that asks all citizens to merge. The model is the national mosaic, individual pieces living side by side: French by English by Inuit-speaker; and, in poetry terms, Language poet by New Formalist. Perhaps not all people like each other, but they *have* to get along, just as citizens of all cold climates have to in order to survive. That is the deal about Canada: It's about compromise, cooperation, and coexistence, just like its parliamentary system. And speaking of governments, let's go back to that Canada Council acknowledgment on every poetry book.

The disparate poets in this volume all partake of the very strong notion that Canadian literature defines the Canadian identity, and this idea is shared by broadcasters and government officials, who speak of how Canadian literature creates (both among Canadians and on the world stage) powerful images of what this country is and means. Canada is immensely proud of its poets. Legislators understand that the making of literature is the making of a national identity—they have put their money on it. Canadian poetry publishers have taken on the task of creating the national imagination, devoting themselves to promoting poets like vowel-obsessed Christian Bök, who stretches the poetry toward acrobatics of sheer language (and gets on the best seller list in doing so), and sense-obsessed Lorna Crozier, who roots poetry in the national tradition of horticulture that she versifies it for its citizens. On the surface these poets haven't a shred in common, but they are the ears and eyes on the national face.

Paradoxically, the Canadian support of its poets may keep the poetry at home. If you are busy defining your nation *to* your nation (often in contrast to your elephantine neighbor to the south), you don't necessarily aim to infiltrate other countries' cultures. This is why American readers (and others) might need a few tips for reading the poems selected by that intrepid proponent of Canadian poetry, Sina Queyras:

Don't panic if each poem doesn't start with a bang. While American poets train for the high diving board, jackknifing into the deep end of the pool, Canadian poets presume that readers will let them wade out until their feet no longer touch bottom. So if you are used to the fast splash of the American poem, a Canadian poem may seem as interminable as a raga is to the listeners of a pop song. In other words, you may find yourself wondering when these poets will get to their points. In fact, there will probably be several points; Canadian time is time unwinding, not time in a flash.

You also might encounter a peculiar brand of Canadian surrealism. The landscape and weather can make for a wild sense of solitude. In isolation, the solo mind plays tricks, and there are perceptual tricks in this poetry. And look out for a mosaic of humor, sometimes ironic and dry as ice, sometimes burgeoning, fresh and almost innocent.

Finally, it may help to remind yourself that one reason this anthology is called *Open Field* is that there are few Big Trees of Canadian poetry in whose shade all Canadian poets must fight to grow. This field is large, open to a sun that beats equally on each species of poem. Like wildflowers, the poems share the same creative soil, the same critical rain, but each has its habit of growth. The botany of this verse holds the possibility of refreshing all poetry in English: it is young, vigorous, and varied, and it carries cultural ideas that might help us all as we ride the storms of the twenty-first century.

Molly Peacock

Toronto

Introduction

> "[Canadian poetry] is not American or English poetry *manqué* but a unique organism: spiky, tough, flexible, various, and vital. Finally its own."
>
> —Margaret Atwood, *The New Oxford Book of Canadian Verse in English*

In a recent *New Yorker* cartoon, two people are standing at a bar. One says to the other, "You seem very familiar, yet curiously different. Are you Canadian?" Readers may have a similar experience with Canadian poetry.

Of course, Canadian poets have been published in American and British journals, textbooks, and anthologies for decades—their nationality most often unannounced. Poets Margaret Atwood, Michael Ondaatje, P. K. Page, Robert Kroetsch, Leonard Cohen and more recently Anne Carson, have long been lauded internationally. However, Canadian poetry as a whole—as a canon—has not achieved wide distribution outside its country's borders.

The anthology you hold in your hands is a response to that gap. It's the result of an ongoing discussion between two poets: me, a Canadian new to New York, and Gabe Fried, a young American who also happens to be poetry editor at Persea Books. In retrospect our meetings were obnoxiously skewed: the expatriate must always decide how much to divorce herself from her country of origin and try to blend into the new one, and how much to wear her country like a badge of honor. I emphasized the latter, carrying Canadian poetry books around in my backpack and slipping them out at readings and salons, on trains and in bars. I prefaced readings of my own work with work by other Canadian poets, filled my classroom with them, and talked about them endlessly.

Discussing literature (or art, or film, or music, or anything you love) with people whose influences, or preferences, you are familiar with, but who have little awareness of your own, can be disorienting. It's fine if you are both equally unfamiliar, but for those of us living north of the one-way mirror that the US/Canada border can sometimes be, the experience is more like: we see you, you don't see us. Most poetic dialogues assume a certain amount of shared knowledge and this imbalance flamed my passion: *You haven't read? You haven't heard?* Fortunately, Gabe was open my to my exuberance (as I have found most Americans to be). After two years of meeting in various bars and cafes in Manhattan and Brooklyn, Gabe usually walking away with one or two books of Canadian poetry under his arm (and I with his favorites, or those newly discovered) the idea for this anthology arose.

One of the first discussions Gabe and I had about the collection was concerning a title, and with that all the clichéd Canadian images of maple leaves, ice, and snow, reared their heads. This was followed—as discussions about the weather usually are—with some talk of the geographical space of Canada: the enormity and variety of it. I was resistant: *We are not our weather! Or our geography!* But later, the phrase "open field" came to me. And it was unshakable. The idea of "open field composition" evokes the powerful connection of west coast poets Fred Wah, George Bowering, Daphne Marlatt, and others, to the American Black Mountain Poets, Charles Olson, Robert Duncan, and Robert Creeley, who visited Vancouver in the early 1960s. Sparks from that meeting are still flying on both sides of the border. But obviously Canadian poetry has grown and changed since then, and this is only one strand of influence. Furthermore, in terms of the literal interpretation, the phrase was limiting. Canada is a cosmopolitan country; its literature mature, complex, cutting edge. Why call up the image of a field? But Gabe liked it, and so did I.

And so, with the title "tentatively" tacked on, I began to read and reread for this anthology. Very quickly it became apparent that Canadian poets' relationships to "nature" are as complex as they are intense. For example, in "Contemplation is Mourning," Tim Lilburn writes, "Looking takes you so far on a leash of delight, then removes it and says / the price of admission to further is your name." The poems invite an exaggerated seeing—a poet's mission to be sure—but there is something sharper here, pushing beyond the limitation of our daily gaze. What must we do to glimpse what the poet has? To venture into the land, shivering under prairie grass "woo-floated from planet-like names and not quite / in things shimmering gravity"? The field as constellation? Night-sky vertigo? Lilburn doesn't so much show his relationship to the landscape as create the physical experience of being in it. I also found this intense looking in the work of Don McKay; self-described nature poet who, in *Vis a Vis: Fieldnotes on Poetry & Wilderness,* says wilderness is "not just a set of endangered spaces, but the capacity of all things to elude the mind's appropriations." Nature here is neither benign nor simplistic, and it is a vital part of our imagination—what we struggle to witness without possessing, and what we want to deny. "You must believe in spring" Jan Zwicky insists, "because the signs are not wrong: you are here." In selections from both Lorna Crozier's "The Sex Life of Vegetables" and Susan Goyette's *The True names of Birds,* it becomes apparent that even when nature is domesticated, it is always surprising. And that surprise can often be surreal—particularly with the women in this anthology. Anne Carson's image of Madame Bovary as the Rocky Mountains, "Cloud shadows rov(ing) across her huge rock throat" and Erin Mouré's "speckled cattle" who all night "snort the seed out of the ground." And who is more surreal, and mischievous than Margaret Atwood? Reminding us with the line "at some time during that hour, though not for the whole hour, I forgot what things were called and saw instead what they are", that she has been thinking about all of this for a very long time, and that perhaps no one is more synonymous with the Canadian landscape than she.

Another aspect of this complicated relationship to nature is an insistence on speaking on behalf of the earth and things on it. Look around you, Christopher Dewdney urges us "The world has become / a spectacle of absence, / a radiant inventory" and everything in it, limestone, fossil, wave particle, has something to teach us. Again, not in a naive, or nostalgic sense—these are not poets who are only looking backward—they are looking at what is in front of them and asking us to as well, and Dewdney has a lifetime of informed wonder to offer. And the repetitious, and radical articulations of Lisa Robertson's *The Weather*: "Days heap upon us. Where is Jane. Looking for food. / Hunger crumbles open. All this is built on loveliness. / We have fallen into a category. / Love subsidized our / descent." Hers is an unabashedly feminist illumination of the relentlessness of weather, power, and indeed lyric. Dennis Lee's *Un*, a book length work designed to elegize/eulogize as much as provoke us into seeing the world around us, is a response to the notion that words have lost their power to move us. If that is true, Lee invents a whole new one to make us appreciate the precariousness of our planet: "In wreck, in dearth, in necksong", he gives us, "in bio in haemo in necro—yet how / dumbfound how / dazzled, how / mortally lucky to be." Could it be that Canadians might have an edge when it comes to listening to the still-wild voices? After all there is simply more wilderness and we are simply closer to it.

In fact, as Erin Mouré makes clear by channeling Alberto Caeiro/Fernando Pessoa's sheep filled pastoral into the still simmering one under Toronto's sophisticated sheen, even the most urban Canadian location is closer to a pastoral landscape than that of most developed nations. Toronto is scored with ravines, Montreal has its mountain, Vancouver lies not only at the foot of a mountain range, but with the ocean lapping at its edges, a hothouse of green. So perhaps in the face of all this space, and our proximity to it, we have room for formal innovation. Some of which is more recognizable: Anne Simpson's graceful corona of sonnets, for example, or George Bowering's *Kerrisdale Elegies* that echo Rilke in his sleepy Vancouver neighborhood, or Ken Babstock's chiseled vernacular, each syllable flexing; or Diana Fitzgerald Bryden, Toronto's most recent flâneur, intricately weaving her narratives, or Todd Swift, politically active expatriate and creative formalist, whose work snaps like a good suit on 5th Avenue, or Saint Denis, or rue du Fleurus. Others, such as the deceptively simple poems of Jeanette Armstrong that come alive like poplar leaves when breath is applied, and Lydia Kwa, who makes us reconsider the page, and what we recognize as poetry, are less recognizable. And as well as the playful confusion about authorship, Erin Mouré's *Sheep Vigil for a Fervent Person* makes us rethink the difference between originary poetry and translation—and who better to do it than one included in this anthology as poet, translator, and transelator—a category of her own.

Imagine the innovative poet, comfortable in her urban center, looking out over all that space. *Expand, expand* we might think, but we are Canadian, and our impulse is more likely to be *connect, connect*. Saying we believe in a net, and we believe in it equally for everyone, has consequences, and we're up for them. We see the interconnectedness in things and our delight, or distress, brims over. Is it a coincidence that long poems have become a rite of passage for the Canadian poet? Book length projects such as Lisa Robertson's dazzling investigation of pastoral in *The Weather*, and George Elliott Clarke's *Whylah Falls*, a bluesy, lyric re-imagining of a black community in Nova Scotia, are often accompanied by a reach that extends as far back in literary time as it radiates forward. And in Clarke's work, as in many other Canadian long poems, there is an added documentary-like quality: *Look*! it insists, *this really happened!* In Nicole Brossard and Daphne Marlatt—two major forces in the strong, experimental feminist poetic found in this country—it is often (although not only) erotic longing that leads to luscious language and expansive audaciousness. For Michael Ondaatje and Dionne Brand it is immigration, family, desire, and in Brand's case, rage—all this with a golden hum that vibrates whole histories onto the page. Projects, such as Christopher Dewdney's *The Natural History* and the late bp Nichol's *Martyrology* are so grand they were published over long periods of time.

Other poets take us to new sites. Mary Dalton's *Merrybegot* to the shores of Newfoundland, with the "swagger / Of a swiler", and Joe Denham's *Flux* tugs us up the Georgia Strait on a seine boat. Karen Solie takes us to meet Walter Benjamin in the "dog-hued" water of a Saskatchewan valley. But Sonnet L'Abbe brings us back to the body and how it fits, or does not fit into our ideas of what poetry is. Fred Wah's *Music at the Heart of Thinking* reminds us that language can be playful: "Le mot juste or just tomatoes? The poem as a field of carrots or stones?" Other poets make the page a journey, or a springboard for linguistic journeying. Is it possible to appreciate bp Nichol's "Cycle 22" without reading it aloud? The same is true of *EUNOIA*, Christian Bök's Oulipian tour de force. If you want to get students excited about language, let them have *EUNOIA*: Devil's Food for the tongue.

Early on in the gathering process the image of a mountain range came to me. I saw poets, not on fields, but on peaks: Zwicky, Lilburn, and McKay on one, Carson, Robertson, and Mouré on another, or Atwood, Ondaatje, and Brand on another. What struck me about this image was that despite what on the surface appeared to be vastly different visions of poetry, each of these poets—the post-modern Mouré, or the lyric McKay—seemed to be looking up from their own work, and the work of their more immediate peers, long enough to appreciate one another's equally spectacular maneuvers. A fitting image given the genesis of this project was in the mutual curiosity about poetic lineage. And perhaps the reason why the title seems so right: Canada is a vast and convivial open field, and these poets make full use of it. This intertextual, adventurous spirit is one reason I hope these poems find their way into classrooms. In a world that is so busy compartmentalizing and downsizing, the expansive vision found here might be refreshing. There is an abundance of excellent writing in Canada, and this slice is designed to serve as an to introduction to it. But the particular blend of formal and innovative work collected here makes for exciting reading, and in my own classroom, it also makes for exciting writing. Another reason these poems need to find their way into students' hands.

But now perhaps I've gone on too long. Although if you tackle an anthology the way I do you've read through the poems and are just dipping back in now because you haven't had enough and want more. Or perhaps you have become a little disoriented. I want to suggest this is a good thing. These poems may show you possibilities you didn't know existed. They might remind you of a place you didn't know you left. Come. Put your ear to the ground.

Sina Queyras
New York City

OPEN FIELD

Jeanette Armstrong

Winds

winds   moving   clouds
past   earth   sky
are   one   moves
around   me   silent   colours
drifting   sometimes   present   dark
with   soft
                                  white
                                  flakes   touching
life   rich   lacework   unknown
            hands   twined   with care
a place   forever   still   tracing   quietly
a line   stretched   to a   horizon
fading   with time   and gently
ending   breath

Green

green   silence   softly
groping   into
          damp   earth   pushes   quietly
draws   tendrils   up   into
rich   dark   interiors
life   turns   to
                    green
reaches   toward   early   light
                    drenching   golden
fills   with
          clean   warmth   dew
soft   summer   breath
                               sends   whispers
                    easily   through
leaves   captures   wind   swirls
          clouds   driving   rain
          washing   dust
                    moisture   and   mystery
swells   twigs   moves
pollen   and   seeds   upward
                    scattering petals   moving
          forests   slumbering in tiny
pods   beginnings in   endless
          emerald   dance   circles

Blood

blood of my people   courses through   veins
coming to me   through dust   rising and falling
across ages   the dust   that is my people
that is the land   rises   a continuous red line
across people   across time   is what we are
the living   pulsing   walking   earth
inside me   this collection   moves   a brief shadow
under the sun   lifted by air   pushed   by the force
of earth   circling   majestically   silent
this small storm   for one intense   moment
this fragile breath   lifted   to twirl   to dance
to fly   the elusive   magic   of weightlessness
catalytic movement   needed   to press   blood
forward   a red liquid   stream   that draws
ground upward   that shakes   earth and dust   to move
to move   a long line   before settling
quietly   back   into the soil

Margaret Atwood

Autobiography

The first thing I can remember is a blue line. This was on the left, where the lake disappeared into the sky. At that point there was a white sand cliff, although you couldn't see it from where I was standing.

On the right the lake narrowed to a river and there was a dam and a covered bridge, some houses and a white church. In front there was a small rock island with a few trees on it. Along the shore there were large boulders and the sawed-off trunks of huge trees coming up through the water.

Behind is a house, a path running back into the forest, the entrance to another path which cannot be seen from where I was standing but was there anyway. At one spot this path was wider; oats fallen from the nosebags of loggers' horses during some distant winter had sprouted and grown. Hawks nested there.

Once, on the rock island, there was the half-eaten carcass of a deer, which smelled like iron, like rust rubbed into your hands so that it mixes with sweat. This smell is the point at which the landscape dissolves, ceases to be a landscape and becomes something else.

Strawberries

The strawberries when I first remember them are not red but blue, that blue flare, before the whitehot part of the wire, sun glancing from the points of waves. It was the heat that made things blue like that, rage, I went into the waste orchard because I did not want to talk to you or even see you, I wanted instead to do something small and useful that I was good at. It was June, there were mosquitoes, I stirred them up as I pushed aside the higher stems, but I didn't care, I was immune, all that adrenalin kept them away, and if not I was in the mood for minor lacerations. I don't get angry like that any more. I almost miss it.

I'd like to say I saw everything through a haze of red; which is not true. Nothing was hazy. Everything was very clear, clearer than usual, my hands with the stained nails, the sunlight falling on the ground through the apple-tree branches, each leaf, each white five petalled yellow centred flower and conical fine-haired dark red multi-seeded dwarf berry rendering itself in dry flat two dimensional detail, like background foliage by one of the crazier Victorian painters, just before the invention of the camera; and at some time during that hour, though not for the whole hour, I forgot what things were called and saw instead what they are.

The Loneliness of the Military Historian

Confess: it's my profession
that alarms you.
This is why few people ask me to dinner,
though Lord knows I don't go out of my way to be scary.
I wear dresses of sensible cut
and unalarming shades of beige,
I smell of lavender and go to the hairdresser's:
no prophetess mane of mine,
complete with snakes, will frighten the youngsters.
If I roll my eyes and mutter,
if I clutch at my heart and scream in horror
like a third-rate actress chewing up a mad scene,
I do it in private and nobody sees
but the bathroom mirror.

In general I might agree with you:
women should not contemplate war,
should not weigh tactics impartially,
or evade the word *enemy*,
or view both sides and denounce nothing.
Women should march for peace,
or hand out white feathers to arouse bravery,
spit themselves on bayonets
to protect their babies,
whose skulls will be split anyway,
or, having been raped repeatedly,
hang themselves with their own hair.
These are the functions that inspire general comfort.
That, and the knitting of socks for the troops
and a sort of moral cheerleading.

Also: mourning the dead.
Sons, lovers, and so forth.
All the killed children.

Instead of this, I tell
what I hope will pass as truth.
A blunt thing, not lovely.
The truth is seldom welcome,
especially at dinner,
though I am good at what I do.
My trade is courage and atrocities.
I look at them and do not condemn.
I write things down the way they happened,
as near as can be remembered.
I don't ask *why*, because it is mostly the same.
Wars happen because the ones who start them
think they can win.

In my dreams there is glamour.
The Vikings leave their fields
each year for a few months of killing and plunder,
much as the boys go hunting.
In real life they were farmers.
They come back loaded with splendour.
The Arabs ride against Crusaders
with scimitars that could sever
silk in the air.
A swift cut to the horse's neck
and a hunk of armour crashes down
like a tower. Fire against metal.
A poet might say: romance against banality.
When awake, I know better.

Despite the propaganda, there are no monsters,
or none that can be finally buried.
Finish one off, and circumstances
and the radio create another.
Believe me: whole armies have prayed fervently
to God all night and meant it,
and been slaughtered anyway.
Brutality wins frequently,
and large outcomes have turned on the invention
of a mechanical device, viz. radar.
True, valour sometimes counts for something,
as at Thermopylae. Sometimes being right—
though ultimate virtue, by agreed tradition,
is decided by the winner.
Sometimes men throw themselves on grenades
and burst like paper bags of guts
to save their comrades.
I can admire that.
But rats and cholera have won many wars.
Those, and potatoes,
or the absence of them.
It's no use pinning all those medals
across the chests of the dead.
Impressive, but I know too much.
Grand exploits merely depress me.

In the interests of research
I have walked on many battlefields
that once were liquid with pulped
men's bodies and spangled with exploded
shells and splayed bone.
All of them have been green again

by the time I got there.
Each has inspired a few good quotes in its day.
Sad marble angels brood like hens
over the grassy nests where nothing hatches.
(The angels could just as well be described as *vulgar*
or *pitiless*, depending on camera angle.)
The word *glory* figures a lot on gateways.
Of course I pick a flower or two
from each, and press it in the hotel Bible
for a souvenir.
I'm just as human as you.

But it's no use asking me for a final statement.
As I say, I deal in tactics.
Also statistics:
for every year of peace there have been four hundred
years of war.

The Moment

The moment when, after many years
of hard work and a long ago voyage
you stand in the centre of your room,
house, half-acre, square mile, island, country,
knowing at last how you got there,
and say, *I own this,*

is the same moment the trees unloose
their soft arms from around you,
the birds take back their language,
the cliffs fissure and collapse,
the air moves back from you like a wave
and you can't breathe.

No, they whisper. *You own nothing.*
You were a visitor, time after time
climbing the hill, planting the flag, proclaiming.
We never belonged to you.
You never found us.
It was always the other way round.

Ken Babstock

First Lesson in Unpopular Mechanics

As a boy, it was a scale-model Messerschmitt
pitched at the wall in a boy-scale rage—
Now? These grown-up middletones, wafflings, shit
flung deliberately wide of the fan. I remember the age
I began to ease off—thirteen, fourteen—
when busting one's stick meant a five-minute major,
and there, in the sin bin, thinking, *what did I mean
by two-handing the crossbar?* Couldn't gauge or
properly reckon what point I had made (hoped
I had made) so kept my caged gaze on the raftered clock:
that massive, red-rashed, free-floating block
where the seconds of my sentence, my stasis, loped
toward zero, zero, and zero in slow-mo.
The thing opposed, absolutely, my re-entering play; its rules,
                                        its flow.

What We Didn't Tell the Medic

When the bike dropped it jammed
a foot-peg into asphalt. Blue
sparks spat off chrome, a dead-stop
catapult sent it clear up and

        we slid right under,
        holding each other.

Time stalled. I stared
at the Honda hovering there—
midair—could have sketched
the scraped tank, the locked
sprocket and axle, forks skewy-bent,
wracked wheel-rims, and lolling
headlight eye. It was an ill-framed
Guernica horse strung
up in the sky.

It felt good though, holding
my friend as we spilled onto tarmac.
I wanted to pull his helmeted
head back and kiss him—
for passing those semis,
for muttering *God* as we fell,
for being there with me, ripping south
on the 401 in a stink of coat-leather
burning, arms apart, like he could
wrestle the back bumper
of the Datsun ahead, and that sky,

that ovoid of impenetrable blue,
pressing in, pressing down, the way
sea-swells can pinch a whole ship, just crack
it in two. My eyes flickered, then calmed;
like a deckhand's last glimpse
of the Grand Banks, they caressed
that porthole 'til it sank.

Palindromic

"The Lord will restore the years the locusts have eaten"
—Leviticus

Christmas alone, by choice, with a tin
    of sardines and bonnie 'Prince' billy
sharpening the blade of the cold on
    the whetstone of his voice. A melee

on the morning of the first of the year
    over who should pay what to who
for the nothing we got the night before.
    There'd been *lots* of it, but it amounted to

loss, I guess is what I mean, given the pain
    and embarrassing, hours-long absences
of someone with someone else whose name
    should stay out of this. Fences

went up around friendships. The exacto blade
    in the thermometer kept snapping
off segments till there was nothing save numbered
    hash-marks seen through a static

of frost. I went for a walk in a parka I bought.
    Zipped up; the city as a fuzzy-edged
dream sequence afloat to indicate thought
    in the head of a smiling protagonist. Cadge

a light from a passerby and now your head's
    the lantern from the 28th Canto
shedding light on hell. "Oh me!" you'd said,
    and no laughter, canned or

otherwise, leavened a life that felt filmic.
    Sometime in March, the plaster over
the tub got pregnant, or Anish Kapoor was snuck
    in to redecorate. Its water burst near

April Fool's and spring arrived stillborn, I was
reading something that hasn't stayed
with me, when the soldiers arrived with shovels.
    It was Mendelssohn screaming at Stoppard,

I think, or Stoppard screaming back, in the letters
    section of the NYRB, about Housman,
was it? As penned by Stoppard?—whatever,
    I remember an exchange of epithets and now's

a little after the fact seeing as the play itself
    never came. One night in May, a barkeep thought
I looked tired and slipped me a pill: I got soft
    in the neck, large in the thumbs, and a spot

of crimson light sang *Agnes Dei* from the foreground
    of my vision's left field. Wall calendars
were argyle socks; all those X's in rows wrapped around
    June under colour shots of designer blenders.

It was like a training regimen to ensure I'd place last
    in the race to accomplish, accrue, attain,
or think straight for a day and a half. I didn't dust.
    Meeting resistance—a door opens onto more rain—

I'd fall back and regroup, reuse the same ringed tea cup
    and liberate a pack of Dunhill from the long ice age
of the freezer. Watched others watch their Weimaraner pups
    grow to full glamour in the park. Massaged

the kinks of appointments from the hurt muscle of months,
    dredged each nightbottom for spare hours
to stare at. Just a therapist and me and a lot of not much
    to work through, more like locating doors

I might walk through if I'd get up and walk. Hypodermic,
    or fifty candies, or warm bath and a pine box:
repeated it all to myself, but self laughed, knew it was weak
    and would linger. Self trips self then mocks

the starfish of limbs washed up in the gravel, another X-
    brace to hold square a day. I read a novel wherein
many were worse off, so read it again, while flecks
    of grey ash mixed with eczematous snow in

the deep gorge between each page. To open it now's
    like opening a text from the Middle Ages, but
you can't, it's glued shut with dead skin cells and sweat. Sows
    at the Ex in August nonplussed with the crowds at

the gate. Too much lost, in ten minutes, at Crown and Anchor,
    and my house keys freed from a pocket while
upside down in those ergonomic gibbets hung from the Zipper.
    So head down for the night on the deep pile.

carpet of clipped-lawn embankment that skirts the expressway.
    Stuff fell in the fall. No one took pictures.
Or painted the scene on wood panel in oil, of the day
    none of my friends and I decided not to go halves

on a driving trip through some of Vermont. I read Frost
    and stayed where I was. Thanksgiving
I thanked someone for the chance to play generous host
    to myself as guest at the bar where, having

been dosed earlier that year, we went back for more.
    By November I was an art installation
begging the question are empty days at the core
    of the question of begging the question.

Borrowed money so's not to be anywhere near Christmas,
    while the snow whitened what no longer
wanted to be looked at. I know now I was missed.
    Then was a different story. I think we're all stronger.

Pragmatist

I was on a tractor in the rain
        when it occurred to me, my paternal
            grandfather was called Henry James

            and cooked meals for men in a coastal
        lumber camp in Bonavista Bay.
The brother of that other James

was William who wrote on matters Spiritual
        and hung with John Dewey. Henry
            James Babstock's brother's name was Samuel.

            So this grandfather, who went by 'Pappy',
        died when I was two. He
was a huge man, gentle, happy,

and given to tossing infants in the air.
        Concerning one's self only
            with the task at hand while temporarily

            ignoring metaphysics has had more
        recent support from the American
thinker Richard Rorty. His name

sounds like a tractor coughing, revving,
        having sat idle in a field in the rain.
            When I was two, and at the zenith

            of one of Henry James's loving pitches—
        up near the ceiling of a white clapboard
house that has since been taken down, or

outdoors above the porch, or 'bridge'
        as he and his wife Alma
               would have called it—I was at the edge

            of something. That descent, and all my
        subsequent nothings and entanglements,
loves, riots, slippages and cries,

could be felt to have happened inside a quiet
        afterthought; a kind of dimming down
            of who I was when I was him and contained.

            Turn now to a book by William James
        on states of religious experience.
I was pulling a trailer onto which

a friend was loading irrigation pipes.
        He was powerful, and beautiful, yet
            far from me, we finished early to a round

            of applause from a bank of thundercloud
        that had reared up over the cottonwoods.
There's a kind of shroud I pull across my life.

Christian Bök

from Chapter A

for Hans Arp

Awkward grammar appals a craftsman. A Dada bard
as daft as Tzara damns stagnant art and scrawls an
alpha (a splapdash arc and a backward zag) that mars
all stanzas and jams all ballads (what a scandal). A
madcap vandal crafts a small black ankh—a hand-
stamp that can stamp a wax pad and at last plant a
mark that sparks an *ars magna* (an abstract art that
charts a phrasal anagram). A pagan skald chants a dark
saga (a Mahabharata), as a papal cabal blackballs all
annals and tracts, all dramas and psalms: Kant and
Kafka, Marx and Marat. A law as harsh as a *fatwa* bans
all paragraphs that lack an A as a standard hallmark.

Hassan asks that a vassal grant a man what manna a man wants: Alaskan crabs, alfalfa salad and kasha, Malahat clams, lasagna pasta and salsa. Hassan wants Kalamata shawarma, cassabananas and taramasalata. Hassan gnaws at a calf flank and chaws at a lamb shank, as a charman chars a black bass and salts a bland carp. Hassan scarfs back gravlax and sprats, crawdad and prawns, balks at Parma ham, and has, as a snack, *canard à l'ananas sans safran.* Hassan asks that a vassal grant a man jam tarts and bananas, jam flans and casabas, halva, pappadam and challah, babka, fasnacht and baklava.

Chapter E

for René Crevel

Enfettered, these sentences repress free speech. The text deletes selected letters. We see the revered exegete reject metred verse: the sestet, the tercet—even *les scènes élevées en grec*. He rebels. He sets new precedents. He lets cleverness exceed decent levels. He eschews the esteemed genres, the expected themes—even *les belles lettres en vers*. He prefers the perverse French esthetes: Verne, Péret, Genet, Perec—hence, he pens fervent screeds, then enters the street, where he sells these letterpress newsletters, three cents per sheet. He engenders perfect newness wherever we need fresh terms.

Relentless, the rebel peddles these theses, even when vexed peers deem the precepts 'mere dreck'. The plebes resent newer verse; nevertheless, the rebel perseveres, never deterred, never dejected, heedless, even when hecklers heckle the vehement speeches. We feel perplexed whenever we see these excerpted sentences. We sneer when we detect the clever scheme—the emergent repetend: the letter E. We jeer; we jest. We express resentment. We detest these depthless pretenses—these present-tense verbs, expressed pell-mell. We prefer genteel speech, where sense redeems senselessness.

from Chapter I

for Dick Higgins

Writing is inhibiting. Sighing, I sit, scribbling in ink
this pidgin script. I sing with nihilistic witticism,
disciplining signs with trifling gimmicks—impish
hijinks which highlight stick sigils. Isn't it glib?
Isn't it chic? I fit childish insights within rigid limits,
writing shtick which might instill priggish misgiv-
ings in critics blind with hindsight. I dismiss nit-
picking criticism which flirts with philistinism. I
bitch; I kibitz—griping whilst criticizing dimwits,
sniping whilst indicting nitwits, dismissing simplis-
tic thinking, in which philippic wit is still illicit.

Fishing till twilight, I sit, drifting in this birch skiff, jigging kingfish with jigs, bringing in fish which nip this bright string (its vivid glint bristling with stick pins). Whilst I slit this fish in its gills, knifing it, slicing it, killing it with skill, shipwrights might trim this jib, swinging it right, hitching it tight, riding brisk winds which pitch this skiff, tipping it, tilting it, till this ship in crisis flips. Rigging rips. Christ, this ship is sinking. Diving in, I swim, fighting this frigid swirl, kicking, kicking, swimming in it till I sight high cliffs, rising, indistinct in thick mists, lit with lightning.

from Chapter O

for Yoko Ono

Loops on bold fonts now form lots of words for books.
Books form cocoons of comfort—tombs to hold book-
worms. Profs from Oxford show frosh who do post-
docs how to gloss works of Wordsworth. Dons who
work for proctors or provosts do not fob off school to
work on crosswords, nor do dons go off to dorm
rooms to loll on cots. Dons go crosstown to look for
bookshops known to stock lots of top-notch goods:
cookbooks, workbooks—room on room of how-to
books for jocks (how to jog, how to box), books on
pro sports: golf or polo. Old colophons on school-
books from schoolrooms sport two sorts of logo: ob-
long whorls, rococo scrolls—both on worn morocco.

Troop doctors who stop blood loss from torn colons or shot torsos go to Kosovo to work pro bono for poor commonfolk, most of whom confront horrors born of long pogroms. Good doctors who go to post-op to comfort folks look for sponsors to sponsor downtrod POWS from LVOV or Brno. Good doctors do months of work on blood flow to show how no form of pox (no protozoon, no sporozoon) clots blood from blood donors. Most Dogon, voodoo doctors, who splosh oxblood onto voodoo dolls, know how to concoct good mojo for octoroons from Togo. Folk doctors cook pots of bromo from roots of bloodwort or toothwort—common worts for common colds.

from Chapter U

for Zhu Yu

Kultur spurns Ubu—thus Ubu pulls stunts. Ubu shuns *Skulptur:* Uruk urns (plus busts), Zulu jugs (plus tusks). Ubu sculpts junk *für Kunst und Glück.* Ubu busks. Ubu drums drums, plus Ubu strums cruths (such hubbub, such ruckus): *thump, thump; thrum, thrum.* Ubu puns puns. Ubu blurts untruth: much bunkum (plus bull), much humbug (plus bunk)—but trustful schmucks trust such untruthful stuff; thus Ubu (cult guru) must bluff dumbstruck numbskulls (such chumps). Ubu mulcts surplus funds (trust funds plus slush funds). Ubu usurps much usufruct. Ubu sums up lump sums. Ubu trumps dumb luck.

Gulls churr: *ululu, ululu.* Ducks cluck. Bulls plus bucks run thru buckbrush; thus dun burrs clutch fur tufts. *Ursus* cubs plus *Lupus* pups hunt skunks. Curs skulk (such mutts lurk: *ruff, ruff*). Gnus munch kudzu. Lush shrubs bud; thus church nuns pluck uncut mums. Bugs hum: *buzz, buzz.* Dull susurrus gusts murmur hushful, humdrum murmurs: *hush, hush.* Dusk suns blush. Surf lulls us. Such scuds hurl up cumulus suds (*Sturm und Druck*)—furls unfurl: *rush, rush;* curls uncurl: *gush, gush.* Such tumult upturns unsunk hulls; thus gulfs crush us, *gulp,* dunk us—burst lungs succumb.

George Bowering

from Kerrisdale Elegies

Elegy One

If I did complain, who among my friends
would hear?
                If one of them
amazed me with an embrace
he would find his arms empty, his own face
staring from a mirror.

Beauty is the first prod of fear,
                        we must
live our lives in.
                We reach for her,
we think we love her, because she holds the knife
a knife-edge from our throat.
                      Every fair heart
is frightful.
              Every rose petal
exudes poison in bright sunlight.

So I close my mouth, and my cry
makes dark music in my belly.
                      Who would listen
who could amaze?
              Friends and beauty
lie waiting in poems, and the god
whose life we once wrote has left us
to muck in a world we covered with grease.

      Maybe I should watch the blossoms
turn to toasted flakes on my cherry tree.

Maybe I should walk along 41st Avenue
where mothers in velvet jogging suits push prams
and imitate the objects of my first lyrics.
Maybe I should comb my hair
the way I did in high school.

In the night the wind slides in from the sea
and eats at our faces;
                         that sweetheart,
she would do anything you ask her,
ask her,
              she'll lie down for a lonely heart.
Night-time's for lovers, maybe, closing their eyes
and pretending tomorrow will be splendid.

You should know that, you adult;
why dont you fling your arms wide
into the juicy air, chuck your ardent loneliness,
bump birds out of their dark paths
homeward to their grieving chicks.

Be grateful—
              sadness makes music, cruel
April tuned a string for you.
                         Moons
whirled around planets waiting for you to spot them.
The middle of the Pacific prepared a wave
to plash ashore at your visit.
                         A radio
switched to melody as you walked by
a neighbour's window.

You should know by now,
                          the world waited
to come alive at your step—
                                  could you handle that?
Or did you think this was love,
                              movie music
introducing a maiden you could rescue?
Where were you going to keep her,
                                  and keep her
from seeing those dreams you were already
playing house with?

When your heart hungers,
                          sing a song of six-
teen, remember your own maidenly love
and the girls that aroused it,
                              make them famous.
Remember their plain friends who danced so well
because they never got into a back seat.
Bring them all back, become a lyric poet again.
Identify with heroes who die for love
and a terrific image,
                          you'll live forever
in your anguished exalted metaphors.
                                  Oh yeah.

But remember nature?
                          She takes back all
worn-out lovers,
                          two lie in the earth, one moulders
above-ground;
                          nature is an exhausted mum,

she cant go on forever,
                           this is late
in the machine age.
                        Can you think of one woman
who gave up on the stag line and turned
to God and a peaceful lawn?

Isnt it about time we said to hell with agony?
Shouldnt we be rich with hit parade love by now?
Arent we really free to choose joy over drama,
and havent we come through looking pretty good,
like a line-drive off a perfect swing
in the ninth inning?
                       It leaves the bat faster
than it came to the plate.
                         Taking that pitch
and standing still in the batter's box is nowhere.

Somebody's talking.
                       Listen, stupid Kerrisdale heart,
the way your dead heroes listened, till
they were lifted out of their shoes,
but they couldn't hear it all, they thought
they were standing on earth.
                    No,
you're not going to hear the final clap of truth;
that would kill you in two heart-beats.

But listen to the wind in the chestnut trees,
the breath of autumn's bleeding,
                       the death
of your young heroes.

You recall the breeze
across from the station in Florence,
where you saw an amazing name by the door?
Remember the clouds pulled off the face
of Mt. Blanc you saw from the morning window?
Why would the wind reach down to me?

Am I supposed to translate that swishy voice
into some kind of modern law?
Make me their liar even as the chestnuts are?

Deesse dans l'air repandue,
flamme dans notre souterrain!

Yes, I know, it is odd to be away from the world,
dropping all the habits you learned so well;
never bending to look at a rose face to face,
throwing your name away,
free of hands that held you fiercely,
laughing at what you once ached for,
watching all the old connections unravel in space.

Being dead is no bed of roses,
you have so much work piled up in front of you
before the long weekend.
But the folks who are still alive are too quick
to make their little decisions.
The spooks, they tell me, can't tell whether they're moving
among corpses or the fretful living.
The everlasting universe of things rolls
through all minds of all ages in every back yard,
and none of them can hear themselves think.

The ones who left early dont need our voices;
they're weaned from this ground as neatly
as we're diverted from mum's tit. But
what about us?
                We need the mystery, we need
the grief that makes us long for our dead friends,
we need that void for our poems.
We'd be dead without them.

Queen Marilyn made silly movies, but she's
the stuff our words are made from.
                                Her meaning
struts along the lines of a hundred lovely books.
Her music may be heard in the gaps in the traffic
of 41st Avenue.
                Her shiny breasts
fill the hands of our weeping poets.

Dionne Brand

from Every Chapter Of The World

today then, her head is thudding
as wet sand and as leaden,

today is the day after, rum soaked,
she went to bed deciding what she wasn't,

didn't she used to be that girl
her skirt razor pleated, her blouse hot iron blown,

who never leaned back, who was walking home
books in hand, the red primers blooding

over her palms, knowing nothing,
knowing no one alive inside her after

knowing nothing
nothing more

she should have stopped and changed shape
conch or mantis,

anyway
prayed

against the concrete wall, bitten the chain-link fencing,
prayed not to turn corners, not to enter any streets,

the moment she sees anything life is over,
she should have memorised the town better

so she would not vanish from it like the hill,
and should have memorised the hill so she wouldn't

notice herself noticing everything
like someone planning to leave

stopped then, and changed shape,
perhaps a woman rounding in uterus

clamping her teeth shut on cloth,
she watches a jar with water and lilies

unable to drink much more,
look one drop sweated from each head,

then is a woman turning inward
only flesh waiting to fall

her head is full of arrows
her head is chained to flight instead,

she's fingering blued pebbles, charred stories swirling in her way,
she's lost the kind of knowledge that makes you last

tells you how to change your shape and only
halfway in everything, halfway shapeless, halfway

different, she should have steered clear of
paper's fragrance, her head is heaving boulders

~

the mouth of the world will open
yawn her in, float her like a language on its tongue,

forgetting
all at once and therefore unfading surprise

at the hard matter of vanity, the relentless conceit
of hatred, surprise, thinking a warm evening

a reasoning gecko in twilight, lemon, a girl's dress
caught in a gate; it can never measure the length of this

tongue of conquest, language of defeat, she's
heard everything before, and would gladly drizzle

into the gecko's string and wall and licked evening,
if she could slip her head, so used to the mind's

enervating sleep on this whole chain for centuries,
she knows every chapter of the world describes

a woman draped in black and blood, in white
and powder, a woman crippled in dancing and

draped in dictators' dreams, in derelicts' hearts,
in miners' lights, in singers' shoes, in statues,

in all nouns' masculinities, in rocks cut out in
every single jungle and desert secret carried

in water's murmur, claps of civilisation, in poets
and workmen on the Panama Canal, all bridges,

barrios, tunnels called history, a woman gutted
and hung in prayer, run on with fingers, sacredly

stitched, called history and victory and government
halls, simmered in the residue of men crying vinegar,

every chapter of the world describes a woman at her own
massacre, carvings of her belly, blood gouache blood

of her face, hacked in revolutions of the sun and kitchens,
gardens of her eyes, asphalt lakes, in telescopes and bureau

drawers, in paper classifieds, telephones, exalted memories,
declarations, a woman at her funeral arrangements, why

perhaps so much of literature enters her like entering
a coffin, so much props up a ragged corpse she thinks,

the dry thin whistle of its mouth, the dead clatter
of its ribs, the rain in its room all day, all night, all

evening, the women walking out of its skull one
by one by one, if she lowers her eyes everything falls

out, if she lowers her eyes from this then perhaps
the rattling gecko could have its say, instead

suspicious, she asks, what gender, as if what
guarantee, if not certainty, how does she hold

a head full of curses, all her days are cracked
in half and crumble,

she can't think of it that way, all tidy like a swept floor
the broom resting out of sight and the unsightly

swept, she can't think of it that way, as just
doings of a passing race, so many clouds of ants

so many fields of fish, and later reassembling
in another tragedy of metal and chemical winds,

so no matter. You see, to circle enemies and
greet them like metropolitan politicians do

is the liberal way, to circle, accept, so
much southern death is a sign of talent

No she cannot speak of this or that massacre, this
or that war like a poet. Someone else will do that. She

sees who dies. Someone with not a hope but a photograph
of someone they loved, walking an Azerbaijan street, a man

and a boy and grief covering their mouth like a handkerchief,
and that feeling in the belly of all gone.

Someone moaning the name of a country, this country, in
Belet Huen, flesh melting into his blood,

in the pulp of human flesh he becomes, blindfolded
and longing for a gateway, a fence, a way out, the way in

which led him by the belly. Someone crawling
at a game of soldiers with a dog's chain and in urine,

"I love the KKK" written on his back and his white comrades
braying and kicking, someone who

the next morning will confess to his skin
and all tribunals saying, no, no, I did not feel that. It was not

race.
Someone scrubbing a plastic tablecloth

in Regent Park saying, "I have talked to God
and he knows, I hope, that I am here."

Scrubbing the plastic flowers off the plastic tablecloth
hoping that god is listening.

Someone whose face you cannot see nor want to, her
dress around her fashionable and stiff with

blood, bent over, as if making a bed on a pavement,
smoothing out a corner of the sheet, she drowns

in the openings of her heart.
Someone in the tumbled rush of bodies cutting out

her own singular life
and the life of a child running with her to a refugee

camp on the Burundi border, caught
in the bulb of a television camera, seen

in her most private moment,
tumbling to the bottom of a mass grave after all her running.

"Assuming we speak of the civilised
world—reflecting a belief in diversity, peace,

economic liberalism and democracy—the choice
is obvious." When editorials dust themselves clean

she dreams noise wrapping the door, disappearing
gunboats steaming toward the middle of America,

bananas floating in the creamy eyes of business
men, old instruction books on the care and discipline

of slaves, not to go too far back, after all not
their fault, no need, plenty enough current

destruction, but then what are we assuming,
left unsaid, if undone, to repeat, Guatemala,

Nicaragua, Dominican Republic, Haiti, Grenada, Costa
Rica, Colombia, Chile, Mexico, all other anagrams scuttling

off that page, inventory is useless now but just to say
not so fast, not so clever, boy, circumnavigating

parentheses may be easy but not the world,
the uncivilised at the end of the day in trucks' dust clouds,

at water holes on the edges of deserts, at moonlight
waiting for crabs to march on beaches, settling into

a doorway's shawl, thinking at last a cup of water, thinking
the blanket stuck around the window will keep the rawness

out, thinking of shoe factory jobs, button factory jobs,
thread, at lines for work, at zones metamorphosing at

borders, moving as if in one skin to camps, smelling
oil wells, sugar burning, cathode smoke, earth drained

of water, earth flooded with water, rivers of slick,
overloaded ferries, all belongings bursting in suitcases

and bundles at more borders, starving in the arms
of offshore democrats with Miami bank accounts,

the tired voting in surrender, those left after the war,
those left after the peace, both feel the same, war or peace,

surrender then if it means powdered milk, if it means
rice, semolina, surrender for airflights out of barren

ice, barren water, barren villages, surrender all parentheses,
all arguments, this world in that one, that one in this

all tangled, the revolutions of an engine turning up refugees,
corporate boards, running shoes, new economic plans

but surrender the parentheses, what are those
but tongues slipping in and out of a mouth, pages

sounding like wings beating in air, what but the sound
of someone washing their hands quickly, beating their lips red.

She looks and she surrenders too, she
surrenders leaning into the moonlight on the verandah,

she surrenders her thoughts and circumnavigations
of her skull to rum, when they ask what became of her,

what was her trouble, no lover, childhood beatings,
loneliness, a weakness for simple dichotomies, poor, rich

black
white

female
male

well if it must be said their details too, and
their missions, wandering through us like a sickness.

She may not leave here anything but a prisoner
circling a cell,

cutting the square smaller and smaller and walking into herself
finally, brushing against herself as against surprising

flesh in a dark room. She
hears the *shsh* of cloth, the friction of her hands.

Even if she goes outside the cracks in her throat will break
as slate, her legs still cutting the cell in circles.

Nicole Brossard

Typhoon Thrum

translated from the French by
Robert Majzels and Erin Mouré

and it takes flight whitecaps typhoon thrum
like an elbow in the night
ray of mores
the world is swiftly dark

everywhere where the mouth is eccentric
it's snowing: and yet this heat long
beneath the tongue, the me curls up emotion
glides ribbon of joy
harmonic eyelids

as the world is swiftly dark
and night turns me avid
from everywhere so much brushes up
that the tongue with its salt
pierces one by one the words
with silence, typhoon thrum

in full flight if I spread my arms
my hair slow in the oxygen
I claim there are vast laws
beyond cities and sepultures
voice ribbon, eyes' blade

tonight if you lean your face close
and civilization stretches out
at the end of your arms, tonight
if in full flight you catch my image
say it was from afar
like a die in the night

and while my sex dreams of daybreak
engorges ecstatic epitheliums
it's snowing and again proximity
I claim it's the aura
or the image asymmetric
of the image in brief full flight

groundswell, image ceremony
my heart is agile
emotion between us
matter of laughter matter too true
and my voice that cracks
in the cold of galaxies

I claim I keep watch in silence
in the rose cold of galaxies
I claim that if the eye is black
it cannot keep watch

everywhere where the laughing virtual mouth
of energy devours dawn disgorges its yes
she cries out as wildly as she comes
tympanum, sonorous mauve
vast laws that lick
the air's depth from afar

in the morning the she glides high
and rivers beneath my skin
are long from so many windings
savoury with women and lucidity
in the morning the river surges swept away
when I touch you
face-to-face in affirmation

Diana Fitzgerald Bryden

Sleepers Awake

Sleepers rise, roll up
their bags, fold coats,
feed dogs. Leave offerings,

mark the gateway
to the garden: a pair
of plastic slippers,

daisy browning on
a broken strap, seen
by the secretary (pricked

by haste she doesn't stop).
North of the church, two men:
one with his back to her,

curved in his wheelchair.
A squirrel near his feet
turns a nut in finicky paws.

The autumn air thick
and warm. The younger man,
providing tension, pulls

the other's arm. Gently, loosens
the dishonoured limb, returns it
to its owner in a smooth, elastic

gesture. Takes the hand,
uncurls the fist, flexes
all its helpless fingers.

The body's still,
apart from this:
closed hand coaxed open

like a flower, a letter,
a window from its sill.
Like a bird's gold wing.

Always, Not Always

Always evening. Always fall
or early winter. Street lights burn;
soft discs smudge into brown

haze. Not always.
Sometimes, in the green
and white of spring

she sat with an old friend
in the park, where mint
made its own season,

cool summer; fragrant
warmth in winter's rain.
He told her of waking

to its smell, subtle blossoming
in tea. Of the fountain where
his daughter liked to play;

the plane's white wings, stains
on shuddering tarmac
where he trained younger men.

Back in the city where they talked
she wakes. Cut-glass
in a strange apartment shimmers

deep, obsessive blue,
fills her eye. In the air,
he told her, land, your loved ones

fall away so easily. . . . It's here,
now, you feel it, faces
turn dispassionate, eyes

glance off you, flicker with some
hostile feeling. But there,
you let it go, hands free.

Except in the whining surge
of take-off and descent
when the earth, its contents,

pull with such force
you beg them not
to let you leave.

Age And The Secretary

The secretary feels age
ticking through her bones.
Flesh slips, self blurs at the edges.

The agonizing creep of time
marked by the computer's clock.
Panic, guilt, at wishing

so much time away. One day
at the gift shop, she says
to a bronze-armed volunteer—

a gilded, crystal-haired
survivor, fore-arm blued
with a forced tattoo—

"Thank god tomorrow's
Friday." A rigid hand grips
the secretary's wrist.

Missing her age (10 years at least),
the volunteer says urgently: "Don't wish
your whole young life away."

And truly, the secretary tries
to follow this advice, but resolve
evaporates before ennui,

and then, the flu:
in the washroom
where the secretary rests

her burning head against
the stall, one woman
tells another of god's love

for her. But as the listener
begins, blossoming, to nod,
agree, and voice her own epiphany,

god's messenger moves on to flatter
new conference attendees.
God's love indeed! The secretary

shakes with fever and disgust,
the second heightened by the first—
she feels its echo in her wrist.

Clinic Day

On the ledge today, the circus.
Observe the secretaries
in their natural habitat—

that is to say,
captivity. Regard
their furtive eating style,

crouched behind their desks.
Speared by a dozen pairs
of eyes. True captives: patients.

Fertility Test

Seeding grit, her body
forks itself above air.
He who examined her—

fed her Lethe's waters,
brought her back—now tells her,
in a room that smells of bleach:

internal scars build up,
adhesions make soft tubes
impassable. *See here*: she reads

the lab report. Stage right,
a residential chorus, following
the same map, nods accord.

"There is a surgical procedure,
sometimes, but . . ." he looks at her.
"In your case, not. . . ."

$\sim$

A well-trimmed door
falls shut, its soft thud
barely audible.

Inside Furama Cakes
a low, internal hum.
Stopped car on a wet street,

windows slowly fogging.
Light, buttery and sweet.
She sits quiet, self-soothing

as her nephew does
to lull himself to sleep.
Hot spots, damage, lit

by one glowing eye.
An inner map
all cul-de-sacs,

blocked lanes and
permanently barred roads.
Well, now she knows.

Anne Carson

Short Talk On Gertrude Stein About 9:30

How curious. I had no idea! Today has ended.

Short Talk On Trout

In haiku there are various sorts of expressions about trout—'autumn trout' and descending trout' and 'rusty trout' are some I have heard. 'Descending trout' and 'rusty trout' are trout that have laid their eggs. Worn out, completely exhausted, they are going down to the sea. Of course there were occasionally trout that spent the winter in deep pools. These were called 'remaining trout'.

Short Talk On
Walking Backwards

My mother forbad us to walk back-
wards. That is how the dead walk, she
would say. Where did she get this idea?
Perhaps from a bad translation. The
dead, after all, do not walk backwards
but they do walk behind us. They have
no lungs and cannot call out but would
love for us to turn around. They are
victims of love, many of them.

Short Talk On Reading

Some fathers hate to read but love to take the family on trips. Some children hate trips but love to read. Funny how often these find themselves passengers in the same automobile. I glimpsed the stupendous clear-cut shoulders of the Rockies from between paragraphs of *Madame Bovary*. Cloud shadows roved languidly across her huge rock throat, traced her fir flanks. Since those days I do not look at hair on female flesh without thinking, Deciduous?

Short Talk On
The Youth At Night

The youth at night would have himself
driven around the scream. It lay in the
middle of the city gazing back at him
with its heat and rosepools of flesh.
Terrific lava shone on his soul. He
would ride and stare.

Short Talk On Orchids

We live by tunneling for we are people buried alive. To me, the tunnels you make will seem strangely aimless, uprooted orchids. But the fragrance is undying. A Little Boy has run away from Amherst a few Days ago, writes Emily Dickinson in a letter of 1883, and when asked where he was going replied, Vermont or Asia.

Short Talk on the Truth to Be Had From Dreams

Seized by a sudden truth I started up at 4 a.m. The word grip pronounced 'gripe' is applied only to towns, cities and inhabitations; the word gripe pronounced 'grip' can be used of human beings. In my dream I saw the two parts of this truth connected by a three-mile long rope of women's hair. And just at the moment all the questions of male and female soul murder, which were to be answered as soon as I pulled on the rope, broke away and fell in a chunk back down the rocky chasm where I had been asleep. We are the half and half again, we are the language stump.

Short Talk on the Sensation of Aeroplane Takeoff

Well you know I wonder, it could be love running towards my life with its arms up yelling let's buy it what a bargain!

George Elliott Clarke

The Student's Tale

Everyone cries for love—
but here's the truth of love:

There was no struggle—
just Uncle Cle uncoiling through the door.

He did three murders—
even their son, wound in her womb.

Aunt Io ruined—a bullet
huddled in her skull.

Pardon my doubts
and my grammar.

But don't *l'amour*
echo *la mort?*

Blank Sonnet

The air smells of rhubarb, occasional
Roses, or first birth of blossoms, a fresh,
Undulant hurt, so body snaps and curls
Like flower. I step through snow as thin as script,
Watch white stars spin dizzy as drunks, and yearn
To sleep beneath a patchwork quilt of rum,
I want the slow, sure collapse of language
Washed out by alcohol. Lovely Shelley,
I have no use for measured, cadenced verse
If you won't read. Icarus-like, I'll fall
Against this page of snow, tumble blackly
Across vision to drown in the white sea
That closes every poem—the white reverse
That cancels the blackness of each image.

The Wisdom Of Shelley

You come down, after
five winters, X,
bristlin' with roses
and words words words,
brazen as brass.
Like a late blizzard,
You bust in our door,
talkin' April and snow and rain,
litterin' the table
with poems—
as if we could trust them!

I can't.
I heard pa tell ma
how much and much he
loved loved loved her
and I saw his fist
fall so gracefully
against her cheek,
she swooned.

Roses
got thorns.
And words
do lie.

I've seen love
die.

Prelude

Shelley's a garden
enclosed.
She don't trust words:
men lie
to lie on top of you.

X, I know languages—
Music or Silence,
Touch or Absence—
that need no words.

My gate's open.
My fruits are pleasant.
Come and taste.

Monologue for Selah

Bringing Spring to Whylah Falls

I cry, in the vernacular, this plain manifesto,
No matter how many fishmen offer you their laps,
Or how contrary you are in the morning,
Or how your hair gleams like dark lightning,
Or how many lies the encyclopedia preserves,
Because, Selah, I won't play them parlour-seducer games—
Card tricks of chat, sleight-of-hand caresses—
Or stick my head in books. I love your raspy,
Backwoods accent, your laughter like ice breaking up!
I'd burn dictionaries to love you even once!
   Selah, I tell myself I come to Whylah Falls
To spy the river crocheted with apple blossoms,
To touch you whose hair fans in mystery,
Whose smile is Cheshire and shadow and bliss,
Whose scent is brown bread, molasses, and milk,
Whose love is Coca-Cola and rose petals
In a ship's cabin soaked in saltwater.
But my lies lie. My colleged speech ripens before you,
Becomes Negro-natural, those green, soiled words
Whose roots mingle with turnip, carrot, and squash,
Keeping philology fresh and tasty.
    You slouch and sigh that sassy, love speech,
And aroused, very aroused, I exalt
Your decisive eyes, your definitive lips,
Your thighs that'd be emboldened by childbirth,
For when you move, every line of poetry quakes,
And I inhale your perfume—ground roses,
Distilled petals, praise your blue skirt bright
Against your bare, black legs! *You won't wear stockings!*

I'm scripting this lyric because I'm too shy
To blurt my passion for you, Selah!
My history is white wine from a charred log,
A white horse galloping in a meadow,
A dozen chicks quitting an egg carton tomb,
But also selfish, suicidal love.
I don't want that!
　　Selah, I want to lie beside you
And hear you whisper this poem and giggle.
Selah, I thought this poem was finished!
Selah, I am bust right upside the head with love!

To Selah

The butter moon is white
Sorta like your eyes;
The butter moon is bright, sugah,
Kinda like your eyes.
And it melts like I melt for you
While it coasts 'cross the sky.

The black highway uncoils
Like your body do sometimes.
The long highway unwinds, mama,
Like your lovin' do sometimes.
I'm gonna swerve your curves
And ride your centre line.

Stars are drippin' like tears,
The highway moves like a hymn;
Stars are drippin' like tears, beau'ful,
The highway sways like a hymn.
And I reach for your love,
Like a burglar for a gem.

Quilt

Sunflowers are sprouting in the tropical livingroom.
Pablo, I am falling away from words.

The newspaper scares me with its gossip of Mussolini and
the dead of Ethiopia.
The radio mutters of Spain and bullets.
Only the Devil ain't tired of history.

Yesterday, I saw—puzzled beside railroad tracks—a horse's
bleached bones.
Roses garlanded the ribs and a garter snake rippled greenly
through the skull.

The white moon ripples in the darkness of fallen rain.
The sunflowers continue in the living room.
The latest reports from Germany are all bad.

I quilt, planting sunflower patches in a pleasance of thick
cotton.
I weave a blanket against this world's freezing cruelty.

Lear Of Whylah Falls

Muscular, maddened, and wrecking cornstalks,
Our Lear totters, interrogates the crows,
Keels, and rags his majesty on brambles.
Felled, green maple leaves tangle in his hair.
Imbalanced by illicit, bitter ale,
He vows he'll slog to the cold Atlantic
To sound the wrinkling and remorseless deep
That shut over the head of Lycidas,
To aquarium his queer brain in brine
Under the tumult and racket of gulls.

    Let Othello sleep now. O, lay him down,
Oceaned in silk sheets and flannel blankets,
Quilts of floribunda (a glimpse of death—
The poor sadness of pine which encloses).
Twine our fallen monarch a crown of vines
And roses (he will be beautiful in death),
And wind beside the Sixhiboux and perch
On rocks and mourn for all humanity.

Lorna Crozier

Packing for the Future: Instructions

Take the thickest socks.
Wherever you're going
you'll have to walk.

There may be water.
There may be stones.
There may be high places
you cannot go without
the hope socks bring you,
the way they hold you
to the earth.

At least one pair must be new,
must be blue as a wish
hand-knit by your mother
in her sleep.

~

Take a leather satchel,
a velvet bag and an old tin box—
a salamander painted on the lid.

This is to carry that small thing
you cannot leave. Perhaps the key
you've kept though it doesn't fit
any lock you know,
the photograph that keeps you sane,
a ball of string to lead you out
though you can't walk back
into that light.

In your bag leave room for sadness,
leave room for another language.

There may be doors nailed shut.
There may be painted windows.
There may be signs that warn you
to be gone. Take the dream
you've been having since
you were a child, the one
with open fields and the wind
sounding.

~

Mistrust no one who offers you
water from a well, a songbird's feather,
something that's been mended twice.
Always travel lighter
than the heart.

Fear Of Snakes

The snake can separate itself
from its shadow, move on ribbons of light,
taste the air, the morning and the evening,
the darkness at the heart of things. I remember
when my fear of snakes left for good,
it fell behind me like an old skin. In Swift Current
the boys found a huge snake and chased me
down the alleys, Larry Moen carrying it like a green torch,
the others yelling, *Drop it down her back*, my terror
of it sliding in the runnel of my spine (Larry,
the one who touched the inside of my legs on the swing,
an older boy we knew we shouldn't get close to
with our little dresses, our soft skin), my brother
saying *Let her go*, and I crouched behind the caraganas,
watched Larry nail the snake to a telephone pole.
It twisted on twin points of light, unable to crawl
out of its pain, its mouth opening, the red
tongue tasting its own terror, I loved it then,
that snake. The boys standing there with their stupid hands
dangling from their wrists, the beautiful green
mouth opening, a terrible dark O
no one could hear.

Cucumbers

Cucumbers hide
              in a leafy camouflage,
popping out
when you least expect
like flashers in the park.

The truth is,
they all have an anal
fixation. Watch it
when you bend to pick them.

Carrots

Carrots are fucking
the earth. A permanent
erection, they push deeper
into the damp and dark.
All summer long
they try so hard to please.
Was it good for you,
was it good?

Perhaps because the earth won't answer
they keep on trying.
While you stroll through the garden
thinking *carrot cake,*
carrots and onions in beef stew,
carrot pudding with caramel sauce,
they are fucking their brains out
in the hottest part of the afternoon.

Onions

The onion loves the onion.
It hugs its many layers,
saying O, O, O,
each vowel smaller
than the last.

Some say it has no heart.
It doesn't need one.
It surrounds itself,
feels whole. Primordial.
First among vegetables.

If Eve had bitten it
instead of the apple,
how different
Paradise.

Mary Dalton

Conkerbells

That winter was cold—Lord yes—
Wind barrelling out of the north
Canvas lifting up off the floor
And conkerbells hanging thicker than
A horse's dong. But that young
Dogger could smell the lick
Of a flame, trailed me and
His sister the length of the back ridge—
No chance of a kiss and a cuddle
Once he tripped in the juniper
Toppled arse-over teakettle
Smack into the boughs of our hot little tilt.

The Doctor

November and a snarling gale.
Out they came in the small hours—
Two red little moon men—
Not the weight of a bag of flour
Between the weight of them. The doctor
Came after the mid-wife, eyed them both,
Barked out his verdict:
Nothing to be done for them,
Was off in a flash. So they
Jammed the stove with junks to the damper,
Stuffed wool from the sheep in a
Drawer from the bureau,
Lined that nest with thick flannel,
Fed them like sick lambs with a dropper.
Six long months they captained
That kitchen, steered those
Two little moon men to shore.

Down The Bay

It's so barren down there
A crow's got to bring
A stick to pitch on.

Flirrup

Fairy squalls on the water.
I'm marooned at the window,
Waiting for the fog man,
Sewing the old black veil.
The Walls of Troy on the floor.
There's Dickey just gone up
The road in a red shirt. He's
Sure not the fog man—
Traipsing along with the swagger
Of a swiler in the spring fat.
Not a feather out of him.
Now he'd be the one to have in
For a feed of fresh flippers,
A taste of my fine figgy cake.

Mad Moll And Crazy Betty

We hated them mad rocks, yes,
Worse even than a hog's nose—
The saltwater hove up out of itself
Spinning out and up like a wild top—
Mad Moll and Crazy Betty,
Snaky with their sea-weed hair,
Slimy and slobbering,
With the water moving over their heads.
That lapping over and over.
A sea drooling for blood.

My One Brother

Well, sure, we both popped
The same day out of our mother,
But look at the shuffle on him—
He's slow as an earthworm
And all caught up with stuff as
Far back as the boar's nuts.
Mark it down—you won't be stuck
For a fine line of old foolishness
Long as he's this side of the clay—
My one brother, maundering on—
The king of pishogues,
The pod auger days.

She

Was as good a gun
As ever was put to your face,
And she could kill anywhere.
All you had to do
Was hold her straight. But
She was miserable saucy.
She've had me shoulder
Beat all to pieces.

Sterricky

Those young gamogues
Fast as a Mobile goat—
They got the horse—
And she a sterricky horse, Moll,
Set in her ways and prickly
As a high-summer teasel.
And they got a spruce bough and
Just give her a few tickles under the belly,
And she give the big kick,
Put the door in and sent the
Barrel of water ass-over-teakettle.
Pure devilment—garrickty, garrickty.
She up and cantered off west,
Not a glance at the garden.
Our eyes out on stalks,
Glad now for the wiggling fence.

The Water Man

At dark, when the waves leapt,
When the wind faffered,
We'd sometimes lay eyes on him.
Salt crusted in his hair,
He swam in under the stages.
Sleek. The eyes of a seal. He
Glistened. Called us out in the dim light
To the sea-eels, the sea-snails
And all that was waving and watery.
His voice like a harp in the wind.
Good-bye to the land.
Skin prickling with fins,
Hands over our scaly ears,
We'd turn to the cliffs and we'd run.

Yet

Moll doll his chin;
Her hair birch-
Broom-in-the-fits;
Chalk and cheese, they said;
Cradle and grave,
They said;
Yet—
You could smell
The smouldering, sparry,
Whenever they met.

Joe Denham

Night Haul

I etch ephemeral sketches in flat, black water,
swirling the pike pole like a sparkler wand,
the steel spear tip igniting fairy-dust krill
as we drift in to haul up our catch.
An industrial gramophone, the hauler
churns a music of creak and moan
over the rumbling whine of diesel
and hydraulics, the echo of our exhaustion.
We sit astride the gunwale, hunched
and awing at the swooping arc of green
the line bends below the surface,
tugging the boat over the set—
till traps stream like marine comets
emerging from the depths in a burst of glow
and morphing back to bare utility
whatever beauty we'd begun to imagine.

Breakfast

Stiff as a crustacean's carapace
we cram into rain gear and stretch
on gloves to the auxiliary's muffled yodel
and the gargle of percolating coffee.
A quick cup and smoke on deck
with some *Nice to see your smashed-*
asshole face this mornin', then toque
and flashlight on, and climb down
into the forty-below-Celsius hold.
Bent into the boat's cramped belly
cold air clasps our lungs in a metallic
vice—crystallizes to ice upon inhale,
melts to mist with each exhale—as we
load totes down through the hole's
narrow mouth, feed it the frozen flesh
we caught and killed last night.

Fo'c'sle Dreams

Too often working, or caught in the pincer
of a karma-charged crab. Last night
I crawled the sea floor, crustaceous. Clawed
through a maze of lost gear: rusting
traps, twisted snaps, line smothering coral.
Lured by the scent of fish feed on the tide
I climbed the limestone cliff it misted
down from; up trap-mesh, in through ring-tunnel.
As I lifted to the lip of the elastic-harnessed
bait cup hung above me
it was empty. That's when the darkness
shuddered. The trap dragged, then sprung
from the rock and sucked me upward,
my calcified body compressed by velocity,
water's weighted pressure. Eighty fathoms
hauled by the force of hydraulics to the surface.

Scotchman Salvage

Don't slip. The bark's been skinned off
these cedars by the grapple-yarder pull
and tug-haul down the Strait: they're slick
as *umbilicaria* lichen after downpour; one mis-
step and the space between logs
will suck me under
and seal. What is it about risking life
to salvage stray gear
that enlivens? Stab the pike pole
into softwood. Inch near. At the front
crook an arm over the tow cable and sink
down onto submerged logs, water
vortexing my waist. One look back
to the boat idling at the edge of
the boom, then thrust the pole-hook
to snag the balloon's frayed line. Spike it.

Setting

Snap it on and the anchor scrapes
over aluminum, plunks down into
the purling wake. The line sinks fast
where it falls. Just past noon, our day
already old, but far from over.
I've done this so many times
that it's mindless, so I drift back—
my arms snapping on traps the way
automated machines assemble things—
to my first day on the sea: panic
in my muscles as I fought the line
zinging past my face, wrestled with each
knot that leapt like a crouching wildcat
from the line basket. Now I sidestep
their pounce, daydream as they pass
of all that becomes second nature.

Gutting

Peel back the squirming tentacles
and slice the beak out like the stem
of a pumpkin. As I flip its head inside-
out, I can't help thinking *sentience*
of a four-year-old child, can escape
from a screwed-down mason jar, emotions
are displayed through shifting
skin colour. The dead, still-groping body
in my hands is dark, its sepia fluid
soaking into my sweater and gloves.
I bring the glinting blade down and
cut the blue-grey guts away, catch
my reflection in the steel-shaft
mirror: guilt-wracked, gut-sick
for two bucks a pound, fish feed,
tako sushi on Robson Street.

Mending

Black mesh torn by the rock shelf's clinging
resistance, its gnarled-tooth gnawing, this trap's
become a sieve all but octopus, Dungeness
and dogfish slip through. Between
strings I take the mending needle
spooled with green twine, stitch
the gaps the way my skipper sealed
the gash in his own palm
when a hook embedded in the line
hauled through his hand and ripped it open.
Everything out here is sharp-edged,
broken. Half our time working with holes
we've no time to mend. I take
each spare moment to tie frayed ends:
reef for tension, knot the twine,
and cinch down tight.

Morning Set

In the morning the languid rhythm
of waves lapping the fibreglass hull
lulls us from dreams of softer beds
to the catacomb dark of the fo'c'sle.
The tired boat tugs its tie-lines,
bow, spring, and stern, then rolls
in waning slumber, groggy in its slip.
The creak of bumper on tire, the wind-
chime ringing of stabey-pole rigging,
even the gulls' off-key mewling
coaxes us back into foggy half-sleep—
till the shrill clang of the alarm clock
and our skipper's coarse, timbral cough
lifts the dream-load from our weighted eyes
and we rise to his footfall and Zippo-flick—
the whine and sputter of the diesel turning over.

Christopher Dewdney

The Memory Table I

Lime, calcium, silica, pyrites,
THESE came to remember.

As there is
a water table
there is also
a memory table.
The shafts
by which we remember
are called
"wishing wells" by some,
and the children
of the memory table
are Baudelaire's
somnambulistic chairs.
Which goes to show
some radio stations
are so flexible
you can pick them up
with a dime.

Radiant Inventory

The world has become
a spectacle of absence,
a radiant inventory.
The sunlight that falls
on the margin of the lake
nurtures a deficit
in its clarity, its violence.
These waves are items are
a description of themselves
in discourse with their changes
through time. The sand
is a finite texture of
self corruption. Everything
interpenetrating, extensile,
at once continuous and discrete.
This sunlight both sustains and erodes
the luminous surface of matter
the precise miracle of life.

Now that I have been opened
I can never be closed again.
The reflection of the sun on the waves
is a shining path to the horizon
a dazzling lucent shuttle
of unknowable complexity.
A cloud over the sun
momentary camera obscura.

And as I move towards resolution
the world abandons its detail
in a theatre at once dark & light
where life is a kind of joyous shade
a shadow over the sun
a dark radiance.

Depth Sounding, Lake Windermere

Suspended
      on the still surface of the night lake
we paddle silently towards the beach.
Its mysterious presence a kind of muteness, an assertion
equivocal to our liquid passage.
On the shore
a stand of birch
becomes a grove of fossil lightning
in the blinding silence
of a full summer moon.

Our paddles conspire purchase
in an invisible plane
glistening, imageless.
Each stroke leaving
two whirlpools,
      whispering vortices which zipper up
a single vocable.
Utterance from
the depths of the lake.

The Immaculate Perception

Consciousness requires the immaculate 'separateness' of objects of its attention. It is necessary that the boundaries of the 'object' are clear, in order to fortify its identity, its distinction from the matrix.

Identity is signification.

Perception, the actual neurochemical process of the nervous system, is not as specific as the *ideal* of signified attention ascribed to as "consciousness". There comes a point, a tactile limen, when you can't distinguish between two fingers and one as they are pressed into your back. This demonstrates a lower-level discrimination limit, an equipment limitation, where the sensory system can't resolve fine detail.

The specificity of consciousness, the 'I' perceived, is also diffuse. It is generated by the same neurochemical process as perception. Specificity in vision, for instance, is a result of the resolution of a mosaic signal within the visual cortex. The mosaic signal is characteristic of the entire nervous system. Its granular nature in vision is revealed by aberrant states, such as 'mosaic vision' in migraines and 'pointillistic vision' as induced by both migraines and hallucinogenic drugs. The diffuse specificity of both consciousness & perception sensuously irritates signified or ideal consciousness.

Another aspect of this sensuous irritation is revealed by certain pathological obsessions induced by two neurotransmitter mimetic drugs, d-lysergic acid diethylamide and methamphetamine. This obsessive behaviour, called *punding*, such as picking hairs out of a rug, cobwebs out of hair, sand out of sugar, dead skin from live or sorting trivial objects according to class, is animated by consciousness in a reinforcement of 'ideal' signified attention running upstream against the 'flow' of the mosaic signal.

The Cenozoic Asylum

Wooden alveoli erect and fragile
in the rarefied air of October, leaves
frosted-glass, rock chapel orange and red.
The sky no longer enclosing us. The sound
of a distant airplane blossoming into clarity
and not enclosed. Eels pulled from
the canal. Even the planets are motile,
hoary with diamonds above the chiming
sunset. She swims alone and naked
in a clear October lake. A white building
stands free and O the spirits look dimly
out from there.

A light Modigliani orange as June evenings
are a pastel rainbow of dreams and mercury
vapour lamps, like giant mantids, just
coming on over the shopping plaza.
The violet and pink light setting tanned
skin aglow. Each muscle a new surrender.
The quiet village streets technologized
by our telephoto insignia, lush nightfall
still after a summer shower. The expectant
interglacial period gardens, their scale-speed
hierarchies squandered by darkness. Stars
arbitrate the carnivorous writhing
of cycads.

The pond magnifies its own refractive
distortion. Spring-fed, the precise internal
branches of underwater plants weave over
the pale, turquoise clay. Milky-green glass,
night conscious of itself, is secreted in large

fragments at the base of the cedars
surrounding the pond.

The elevator at Niagra Falls opens
to gardens on both levels. Floral dais.
The red image of the setting sun, opalized
through cirrus haze, reflected from car
windows. Insects, charmed particles
of dusk, orbit the sodium vapour lamps
above the expressway. The streetlights
menace the metal scuttling beneath
them like polished electric beetles.

Summer glen of green grass and tall cedar
and spruce. The spider's web beaded
with morning dew, an abacus
in the gravitational field of the moon.

The envelope of consciousness surrounded
by an aureole of dissolving nucleotides.
Glad solstice of the internal summer,
a tender explosion in the last enclave,
annihilate. Her nipples stiffen, flakes
of come peel off like cellophane. Her
delicate white legs unfolding.

$\sim$

Each figment profound the music
is blown glass and cruelty turning
on some spit. Fired by the vast machinery
of the stars and their mysterious burning.

Each house encloses a novel dusk, turning
off all the lights. Windows open on both
sides to giant trees, still as dew
in the summer night. Water nymphs
enclose themselves in warm limestone
streams. Fireflies pinpoint cool luminous
ideas in the neural foliage of dreams.

Genital clusters. Leaf grotto.

A translucent Saturn, large as the moon,
ascends behind the vacant observatory.
In starlit fields unearthly children rehearse
an absent embrace.

The underwater archetype of your eternal
existence in sunlit brook chambers. Bend
sinister freed the broken consort.
And we built a temple in the warm night
air. The enormous hollyhock flower looms
paraboloid in the visual scan of the hover
fly. With cells shining gold rings and thin
amulets around the corporeal swarm.
The occasional giant thrusts through
the canopy, branches bending
in the rainless wind of a nocturnal heat
storm. The body is assembled around
the perceptions. Tiny iridescent bees.
The wind soft thunder in our ears. Reagent
command the word transcribed. Tactile
revelation of the optical sector. The anvil
tops of cumulonimbus graze

the stratosphere, moonlight high over
the storm witnessed by a small passenger
airliner lost in the nineteen thirties. Sucrose
in the infinite capillary network of the horse
chestnut, its sub-canopies dangling in ever-
rising cascades of green. Leafy strata under
which a forest sylph wends, so delicate she
could have been a rumour written in smoke.

Rivers of cool air flow in slow-motion
cascades down the ravines. The heavy air
slides beneath trees as bats inverting flicker
darkly through desire. Fascination drove
them into the shade. Aero-delta over
the river a shock-wave of mist.

One pure burning heart.

The body is a slow fire, an infra-red jungle
of thermal contours. The sun spiking
triangular fossil-jawed, the grain is blonde
and shimmering. The evening sun on a lone
crab-apple tree halfway up the side
of a bleached grassy hill, the blue windy sky.

Susan Goyette

The True Names Of Birds

There are more ways to abandon a child
than to leave them at the mouth of the woods.
Sometimes by the time you find them, they've made up names
for all the birds and constellations, and they've broken
their reflections in the lake with sticks.

With my daughter came promises and vows
that unfolded through time like a roadmap and led me
to myself as a child, filled with wonder for my father
who could make sound from a wide blade of grass

and his breath. Here in the stillness of forest,
the sun columning before me temple-ancient,
that wonder is what I regret losing most; that wonder
and the true names of birds.

This Contradiction Of Passion

If your husband owns a rifle company, you must face facts.
There will always be ghosts. The ghosts of rifle victims follow
you out of your bath, clinging to your nightgown. And the ghosts

of your husband's hands, the contradiction of his passion,
his thin finger tracing your lips, touching your tongue,
and the same finger squeezing a trigger. Wanting to squeeze a trigger.

And if you're a sculptor you're obsessed with the human body,
and must face faults. There will be an arm longer than the other,
a thigh more muscular. But that vision you've seen, that slender

body of spirit with its feathers and wish bone hides beneath
those flaws and day after day you must chase it. Whittle and chisel
after that image you know must be true. When you finish,

your work is in powder, in dust that you sweep up and store
in matchboxes. Maybe you'll swallow it, mixed in your tea
and it will awaken something in you that doesn't yet have a name.

Despite these facts, these faults, I have licked the fingers
of a man who knows the secret steps of stalking
and can follow me anywhere. I have sculpted him here

behind the shadows I keep casting. This is my contradiction.
I still want him. I have swallowed the powder of his bones,
slept with his words beneath my pillow. It's the weight

of his body on mine when I lie in his traps;
his teeth, the gentle tracks they leave on my skin.

The Moon On Friday Night

                                      erased all paths to Saturday
and swept up footsteps from the day before. It coaxed buttons
to the lips of buttonholes and whispered, 'you're beautiful,
so beautiful,' to women who speak the vernacular

of loneliness. Softly it slid into the hands of the men
they were with and lent its light to everything they touched.
'See,' the moonlight seemed to say, 'there are so many ways
to be naked and so many ways to be far

from home.' The light reminded the women of songs
they knew, songs written to gauge distance. Later,
still later on this island of Friday night, they sang
those songs under their breath as they bent

to tie their shoes. And they stayed bent long after
their shoes were tied, hearing the wind for the first time
caught in a bucket of baby teeth. It was then they remembered
they were toothfairies, medicine men, and their children's

mouths were empty. They knew of light switches, window
blinds, they knew to throw sand on fire, to blow
at a candle, but this light, this light they knew nothing
about so they carried it home with them. And now they wish

they hadn't. It lights up corners they'd kept dark, lights
their words and gives them new meaning. At night,
they hold their husbands' hands to their mouths.
'Know this light,' they pray, 'touch me with this light.'

The Mythology Of Cures

The only person I've seen all morning
is a man in a long black raincoat, crossing
the street. The blue jays are wet
and sulking in the maple. March.

If he had come to the door selling a bag of cures, cures for
    anything. If he had
a trunk full of roads, long twisting roads that lead anywhere, I'd
    have been tempted.

My daughter knows March the way farmers know
their land. The way they look to the oaks
on the horizon to remind them of something
they mustn't forget. The way she notices crocuses.

The mythology of cures. I could rub the tail of a black cat over my
    eyes to ease
their ache. And rebuild this house to strengthen it. This time I'd
    lay the slender bones

of my great aunts into its foundation. Build it with the secret
    those sisters still
whisper. That would keep me here, listening. That would cure me
    of my travel lust.

The mailbox is spilling over with seed
catalogues. Stargazer Lilies are on sale,
Sweet Williams. She has a special
stick for rescuing worms drying on the pavement.

This season is a breech baby, so sure on its feet and winter, on its
    back, lies moaning
and hot. I spend days writing of my husband, with his paint
    flecked hands. This man,

I think, will forecast change, he can picture furniture moved
around, walls torn down. I write of our garden, the borage I'll
    grow to steep and drink for courage.

She too was breech. I coaxed her with song
to turn, rubbed my hardened belly
but she knew where she wanted to be;
her head always pressed against my heart.

Can we know each other too well, he asks, walking blindfolded
    through our tunnels
of conversation. Are we finishing each other's sentences? I know
    enough not to

answer and to carry witch hazel for his bruises. The books I read
    are overdue, each
day costs me something. I look up his name. It means rhythm. A
    slow, steady beat.

What big eyes you have, she whispers
to her nightmares. What big ears. Some nights
she slips too far into sleep. Spring gets locked
in a suitcase marked for morning.

Another morning, and somewhere another tiger, killed for its
   whiskers.
The cure for toothaches. I'll create the mythology for this house.
   Trust me.

Eat your porridge, your chicken soup. And on paper first, I'll
   answer him.
I don't know you too well, I write, you still surprise me. This, the
   cure for silence.

In This January

This must be the month when someone decided
to make months; to count sunsets and full moons and only give it
so much time. And though Janus looks both ways, this January

is intent only on winter's face. It cups and kisses it
on the forehead, on the eyelashes. Why would winter
ever want to leave, if all that attention kept up.

I pass a half-built church on my walk every morning
and every morning I'm filled with the envy thinking of the dreams
the people building it must have. My dreams are shoeboxes

filled with bones from my feet. When I wake it's with a mouthful
of mother-may-I's and the taunting of another day,
daring me to take a step as it pulls the walls up even higher.

No, it doesn't look both ways, it makes me do that.
This house is a maze of those bare walls, perfect
for showing home movies on. And I've become the projector.

Lydia Kwa

from Roadbook: Suite of Hands

You must exist. Writing this book depends on it. It has occurred to me who you are. Someone who does not need to be liked by me. When you chance upon this book, what will you discover in its codes? I would hope for your curiosity.

My hands are ravaged by a severe eczema. All the lines on my palms, even my fingerprints, are obscured underneath a searing fire of burning skin. Surfaces disappearing. The haunting occupation began four days before 9/11, when an acquaintance I deeply admired killed herself.

The affliction is not new, only made blatantly visible and painful on the skin. Eczema is ugly, monstrous. Or so I had thought. At least there is little room left for concealment. The beauty of imperfection outlasts the beauty of surfaces.

Others have alluded to this: reality as dream, and dream as truth. I will call this a dream roadbook. A record of an itinerant. The one I often refer to as "she". Do you share similar symbols, if different dreams? I do not ascribe to Freud's notion of a universal set of interpretations, that each literal act or object translates directly into the same meaning. Rather, I am more interested in the textures of details, how they belong in a landscape shifting and alive, constantly interpreted and transformed by change.

You must exist. Like me, in a multiplicity of voices erupting and tinged with longing and tragedy. Write me back if you wish.

~

itinerant

making journeys from place to place
a plan or record of a journey
a road book

~

In a dream suite, she realized she was without hands. The arms were there, familiar, easy, so that some part of her routine intelligence insisted on the truth of hands. Her eyes saw them, but they existed only as phantoms without the will to search for occupation.

While wandering through the first room, she sensed grief creep into her, one memory stretching into another. Tenderness a fleeting pulse from the centre of her chest. She glanced at a small dark table in the far corner, at its blue glass bowl choked with apricots, their skins fresh and waiting.

The sight of vulnerability.

But I didn't believe in my own touching, she whispered at the ash-grey walls, suspecting someone might hear her. Someone she could bruise with her hands, if she still had them. Someone walking around in a different dream suite, whose own mind had erased some other aspect of the body's original freedom.

Soon I'll know myself from having lost, losing until there's nothing left. She imagined each body she had stroked and rejected, until the memories ached at her wrists.

phantom, n.   hand, n.

   a deceitful appearance   *a worker*
   an immaterial form   *influence*

phantom, adj.   hand, v.t.
   illusive   *manipulate*
   spectral   *transfer*

~

I imagine her
staring into
porcelain echoes
wanting to choose

the tap drips
grief is slow
she runs
water into the sink
immerses her wrists

one last cool
reprieve

quick cut
to end pain
bloodied water
soaks deeper
into the earth

what was the day like outside?

where did her mind drift to?

~

What she had read in a book picked off the shelf of a bookstore. The quote entered now through the deeper door of sleep, and stood solitary in the shadows of the next room.

There are the raised arms of Desire, and there are the wide-open arms of Need.

In the corner of dark mahogany panels, she squatted as if waiting for the train, the seventy-two hour one from Xi'an to Urumqi. She squatted to listen better to the woman pacing the floor above her. That creaking presence, anxiety seeping through rhythm. Until the beat of that other's life paced in her mind, heavy and measured.

It was a man who wrote that: the primacy of Desire, the spontaneous gesture of Need. Nothing thinks as clearly as the body.

She raised her arms to the ceiling, trying to reach the woman who paced. How could she bruise this truth past the boundaries of her guarded life?

In a different dream, there was the meaning of light and air. Laughter, long before there had been reason to forget the beauty of apricots in a blue bowl. In a different dream, the woman above her existed in the same room as her, also squatting to wait for trains.

She was still, sensing the impending journey travel towards her from the feet up.

~

handicap, v.t.

    to impose special disadvantages or impediments upon

(but I would still want to reach into the emptiness
      with an invisible pair of hands)

~

*It is only for convenience that we speak of it as a "traumatic memory."
The subject is often incapable of making the necessary narrative which
we call memory regarding the event; and yet (s)he remains confronted
by a different situation in which (s)he has not been able to play a sat-
isfactory part, one to which (her) adaptation had been imperfect, so
that (s)he continues to make efforts at adaptation.*

                              Pierre Janet, 1919–25

Hysterics suffer mainly from reminiscences.

             Sigmund Freud and Joseph Breuer, 1895

*All the phenomena of the formation of symptoms may be justly
described as the "return of the repressed."*

                          Sigmund Freud, 1939

~

wakened
uncurl stiff
imperfect frond
deadened night

flying fish
triple eyed

the anonymous ones
buried under debris
twinned towers
of desire and violence

departed
species othered
not us not them
label wastage

but still
memory struggle
wants
recovery of lost syllables

who and what
fingers and fins and frogs

can I hear
is it possible
they call out

but I could not save her
nor them

the collapsing ache
of strangers lost

The red room. Large and echoing. Without the pretence of painting or photographs. Frames left hanging after theft.

She looked out of a window, and in the distance at the edge of the world there was a vision. It travelled towards her slow as a breath exhaled. She walked out of the room onto the dusty streets. A walled city, yellow bricks carrying sunlight in their pores, a hundred feet high.

I will send her a letter. Reconciling herself to this sojourn. Thirty more paces, she arrived at the edge of a courtyard, defined by a low mud wall. Warriors, all men, in sea green breastplated armour and helmets. Their arms united in sweeping the solid arcs of defence.

She recognized the moves, the muscled art. She turned to address the feminine man, *I am familiar with this but it is the ornamentation of temples I'm more interested in.*

Behind the warrriors, a low temple roof. Paler than the breastplates, a faint turquoise border of ceramic reliefs, curls and waves, ancient secret.

~

does the hand remember
the first time
it reached

breast's rich
satiation

mouth's confession
sucking trust

the reach for
entanglement
the tilt
of desire

?

Sonnet L'Abbé

Reaction To What You Said

A fierce calmness. Heat rises a bubble to the surface,
two. Baby orbs hover on the sweet pool's face

then pop. Pop. Lightness comes together to sound
its disperse. Makes way for the next round

of roundnesses amid the liquid. Red, somewhere.
Fuel to the fire. Pain without a nerve to tear

through. Shimmer at the film simmers from its depth,
the roil and rumble turning over, space tests its breadth

in kick thrash gasps. A fist in the soft wall.
A heel in the flesh. Contracts and expanses. Swells

that crest and break in a wash of horsepower,
anger like a motor carrying, a motor hauling, shower

of meteors splashing hot crowns of plasma
way up there, somewhere a layer of my atmo-

sphere is absorbing a rain of shrapnel, cushioning
shards like broken glass pushed into an ocean.

The flush of soft swirls ebb and eddy, fractals
of cause and effect. The knock of one molecule

on another sending single clicks curling, tendrils
of a hard slap on distant skin spiral and cool

then are picked up at the helictical core,
and hibernate in its genomic fold until once more

some jagged trauma shakes the cone of seed. We need
to burst our violence into sparks of light, or bleed.

Freestyle (Why They Don't Like Rap)

The rhythm scares them.
It's too much like propaganda,
not enough like a march,
its anger too audible,
its public enmity far
too focused and verbose.

Our boys sure can't dance,
nyuk, nyuk!
like house letters,
like a fucking badge.

Those strange slurs, some
consonants disappearing,
ghost words, code
among those who openly own
their unsold flesh.
Old souls on speaking terms.

They'll call it anything but ours.
They'll call it anything but art.

The Jacksons go supernova
interpellating us all
into the rhythm nation. Then
another expensive education wins
a TS Eliot prize for saying anew,
not me.

"You speak so well!"
Chris Rock wants to crack
skulls. He won't stop
saying motherfucker. Pryor's
propped up somewhere,
drooling some garbled hope,
still crass as hell.

Theory My Natural Brown Ass

I've paid for too many degrees,
posited too many historical positions,
made too many semiotic apologetics,
forwarded far too many feminist responses
to too many textual materialities

to have an ass this big.

In theory, my ass
does not signify.

But this insistence of the body,
this non-linguistic expression
of inertia and caloric lust,
is a corporeal truth that mental exercise
can't deconstruct.

Or is it just an inverted absence?
The presence of the lack
of any Aryan heritage?

I'm the post-colonial girl
who went abroad and squatted and lunged
while the maid, snapping out
wet laundry, watched.
Skinny brown bitch, was what I thought!
The poor men looked at my ass
like it was a pair of Boston Cremes.

But I was raised
on white girls' dreams.
This juicy back might fly in hip hop,

but I meant to fit
into tinier social circles,
and JLo's butt's already taking up
two stools at the representation bar.
Missy E's already gone
bonh bo bonh bonh
all the way to the bank.

My ass doesn't give a shit
that my mind is post third wave.
It is imperialist, a booty-Gap,
expanding into a third space: the place

beyond my seams. Who cares
that sizes are all 'seems' anyway:
you shop, you walk
the slippery significatory slope
on which an 'S', 'M' or 'L' might fall.
The mall

is the spatial organization
of desire, I know, but
does that make my ass look small?

from Dumb Animal

Uh

The shyness, the delay to say
I'm thinking, I'm processing,
the silence before the words
string into coherence I can't leave
unfilled, all my ignorance,
the mice scurrying in the maze,
please wait while the images
load, sound saying I'm not
dumb

or the coyness, the delay to say
I'm answering, when I'm processing
the first thought into a string of words
less hurtful, less assessing,
less revealing of the blunt fact
of my unkindness, all my interiority,
the scurry to hide it behind my back
please wait while I remember
your heart, sound the safety on a sharp
tongue

Ah

An open moment,
a prolonging
of notice without
reaction, a downward
fountain of data, filling.
Unclosing, throat's
wholeness wide, to swallow
the thrall of all of it:
full bulge of gulp
held—

not undulating, no
void vacuum
pursuing the moving,
present cud through
a human tunnel.

Sustained hum,
sustenance
pouring, not pulsing.

Rinse without erosion,
flush without the closed
push of peristalsis.

Clarity
not needing blur
to know itself.

Oh

(((((O)))))

this o is my throat
this o is my oh yeah
this o is my really
this o is my credulousness

((((O))))

this o is my soundful closed
this o is my politeness
this o is my mask
this o is my feigned interest

(((O)))

this o is my I see
this o is the shared place
this o is my sympathy
this o is my mistake

((o))

this o is my aha
this o is my incredulousness
this o is my startling backward
this o is our otherness

(o)

this o is just o
this o is symbolic sound
this o is the presence of nothing
this o is common ground

o

this o is my lips
this o is my gentle kiss
this o is my suckling
o my greedy tenderness

oh
uh-oh
oh

Dennis Lee

from Un

inwreck

In wreck, in dearth, in necksong,
godnexus gone to fat of the land,
into the wordy desyllabification of evil—small
crawlspace for plegics, 4, 3, 2, 1, un.

slub

I want verbs of a slagscape thrombosis.
Syntax of chromosome pileups.
Make me
slubtalk; gerundibles; gummy embouchure.

icecaps

Icecaps shrink in the brain-
rays; noetic
infarctions; clots in the tropic of hominid.
Synapse events on the pampas, while
consciousness voids itself in the bowl of sky.

inlingo

In scraggy lingo lost,
high mean-
times petering, thickets of
lex & scrawn:
split for abysmal, hopalong
underword, head for no exit,
grapshrapnel yore spelunking.
Fractal untongue.

dolly

Clone pastoral.
Data made fleece.

Wisdom sub-
rupted; brain on a breakaway nobel bender.

tothis

What hank, what
hanker, what heirloom?
what telltock prayer? what plea?

One unmutated child among the fallout.
One totem, intact in the ooze.

hang-

Hang-
heavy heart, how
crippled you venture. How
hobbled you roam. Into the wake-up and
die of it—hang-
heavy dawdler, dis-
consolate clinger: burrow & sing.

gone

An earth ago, a
God ago, gone
easy:

a pang a lung a
lifeline, gone to
lore.

Sin with its
numberless, hell with its
long long count:

nightfears in
eden, gone eco gone
pico gone home.

herald

Bad
splat of
ontic roadkill.

Heraldic
alley grunge.

history

In cess, in dis-
ownmost, in ripture,
in slow-mo history cease,
in bio in haemo in necro—yet how
dumbfound how
dazzled, how
mortally lucky to be.

hiatus

And the unredeemable names
devolve in their
liminal slouch to abyss.
I gather the crumbs of hiatus.

The blank where *evil* held.
The hole called *beholden*.

That phantom glyphs resound, that
lacunae be burnished.
That it not be leached from memory: once,
earth meant otherly.

bambi

Goldilocks: bambilox: *fress*. Harsh
tunes for bad times.

Sahara of song.

word

Lost word in the
green going down,
husk of a logos,
crybaby word, out
dragging your passel of absence—
little word lost, why in the
demeaninged world would I
cradle your lonely?
You, little murderer? You, little cannibal dreg?!

lullabye

Lullabye wept as asia
buckled,
rockabye einstein and all.

One for indigenous,
two for goodbye,
adam and eve and dodo.

Fly away mecca,
fly away rome,
lullabye wept in the lonely.

Once the iguanodon,
once the U.N.,
hush little orbiting gone.

youwho

You who.
You who never, who
neverest, who
ever unart.
You who summon the watch, who
hamstring the seeker, you who piss in the wine:
with this jawbone this raga this entrail,
with this pyrrhic skiptrace.
You who egg, who
slag, who un, who

Tim Lilburn

Contemplation Is Mourning

You lie down in the deer's bed.
It is bright with the undersides of grass revealed by her weight
 during the
length of her sleep. No one comes here; grass hums
because the body's touched it. Aspen leaves below you sour like
 horses
after a run. There are snowberries, fescue.
This is the edge of the known world and the beginning of
 philosophy.

Looking takes you so far on a leash of delight, then removes it and
 says
the price of admission to further is your name. Either the desert
                                    and winter
of what the deer is in herself or a palace life disturbed by itches
 and sounds
felt through the gigantic walls. Choose.

Light comes through pale trees as mind sometimes kisses the body.
The hills are the bones of hills.

The deer cannot be known. She is the Atlantic, she is Egypt, she is
the night where her names go missing, to walk into her oddness is
                to feel severed, sick, darkened, ashamed.

Her body is a border crossing, a wall and a perfume and past this
she is infinite. And it is terrible to enter this.

You lie down in the deer's bed, in the green martyrion, the place where
language buries itself, waiting place, weem.
You will wait. You will lean into the darkness of her absent
body. You will be shaved and narrowed by the barren strangeness of the
deer, the wastes of her oddness. Snow is coming. Light is cool,
nearly drinkable; from grass protrudes the hard, lost
smell of last year's melted snow.

Stability

You go into the shy hills.
You are sorry
Large winds are falling inside things.
Momentum from Descartes leaning into fire, wax melting in his
    hand.
Maelstrom of concupiscence dampening in the evening of things.
And against this the world turns too beautiful.
You elope into grass,
into hills' heavy light, into winter pale grass.
Res extensa, reliquary of chaos.
The hills are dark, mid-Atlantic, wilderness made
                        by no one thinking about it.
Clouded with the jived, ambidextrous eccentricity of the grass.
Lean room for the ear, stone in the sea,
coyote-lit, the hills.
Sit on wind-snapped poplar;
quill-brown hummocks and saucers, grass
                        a museum of violations of expectation.
First moths shake from snow, history flows
to its lure at the thinnest point
on the mainland of the invented life.
You wait in the cave of the hills.
You have been stared at by deer and
must grow smaller.

How To Be Here?

I

Desire never leaves.

Looking at wolf willow bloom,
streaming through plushlands of scent toward the feeling
of its yellow,
self breaks up, flaring in stratosphere.
Looking undermines us.
The world and its shining can't hold our evaporating weight.
The world or what is there goes away
as we enter it, goes into halls of grass where torches of
darkness burn at noon.
Goes into light's lowest mind.
Leaving us, woo-floated from planet-like names and not quite
in things' shimmering gravity, alone in wide June air.
All-thumbs intensity that feels like virtue or music.

The Form quivers in the deer.
She doesn't see me; I'm lying barely above grass on a plank
between fallen
poplars.

Hot day, slow wind; I lift on the cam of rhizomes.
The light behind her light is a shell she's just now born out of.
The Form is the doe's ease within herself.
I came from there.
If you dug with small tools into radiant belts round her shoulders
you'd come to a first settlement of the soul, stroke pottery bits, put
your tongue on old cinders and remember.
Tears will take you part of the way back but no further.

II

You wake, say, inside a large mosquito net,
you're away from yourself, older, near a desert perhaps,
air cool, dry, cloud of small sand, everything seems far
away, North African, night ancient, hard to read, you
look through the flap and see something bent toward a fire,
sparks low round it, stocky, sitting on its man-calves, force, tiptoed.
It is desire.
Yes, adding stick after stick, it seems,
managing in its naked hands
the reins of occurrence,
charioteering the will—horses of night.

You want to walk in the dark garden of the eye of the deer looking
        at you.
Want a male goldfinch to gallop you into the heart
                of the distance which is the oddness of other things.
All would be well.
Desire never leaves.
Mercury's flower, a ghost-hurtling.

A mirror held before the spiritual wind
that blows from behind things,
bodying them out, filling them with the shapes and loves
of themselves.
You want that
and all else that shows in the bright surface polished by the lunge and
                prowling of your desire.
You don't know what you are doing.

III

Desire tells me to sit in a tree.
I live alone, mentally clothed in the skins of wild things.
Desire sways ascent into me.
I look, I look: bull-necked hill, blue sweetgrass in hollows.
Knowing is a bowing, a covering of your face, before the world.
The tree's white tallness praises through me.
What receives the bow?
I am seduced by the shapeliness
            of the failure of knowledge.
My name in religion is the anonymity of grass.
I practise dying.
Each day, the tutor, old man, eros, repeats the lesson,
        I wrinkle my brow, my tongue protrudes.
Outside the window one chokecherry in the bush,
in a thicket of gooseberries,
adds a weight and compression of darkness under the sun
                    that is perfect.

Sunflowers At Prime

for Honor Rogers

Numinous, golden as Cappadocian bishops,
ikon ectomorphic, the sunflowers, penumbraed,
Athos-still, recollected as storks
asleep on one green leg, raise their one hand,
palm out in Pax.
The palm, ikonostasis benedictus, like the palm of a simpleton
saint, whose mind is a blister of light,
                                        is a palm, note, in which an eye
might be expected to form and beneficiently wink. It,
the sunflowers' palm, opens, exposing helianthus giganteus'
purple eidetic disc, an ur-mind undifferentiated from body, opened
                                                            in blessing
out, empty toward the golden burst,
composed this vegetable eye, mauve
in the middle of an opened, yellow hand,
blank in adoration of the six a.m. light.
Pax Mundi, pax eros,
yes dears, pax in the court of Re,
Sol Invictus, Pax,
temple virgins of the yellow star,
the holy useless ones, sisters.

Their song. The musical equivalent
of yellow for which mad Vincent thrashed his brain
until his ear was insane and he tore it by its roots.
Yellow. Praise song of yellow. Spirit contralto, bel
canto groan of yellow's deepest longing,
octaves over the stones' tum-tum,
earth-beat, over the range of dogs
                            eiyah   eiyah   aaaah.

The song of yellow vastly more soundless than the wholly imaginary
phlfff of white butterflies in pig-eared cabbage. Yellow.
Yellow. The chant, yellow's singing. The song the sunflowers
are singing when they sing yellow,
yellow, yellow in their swag skulls swollen thick
with July's degrees, a chant interiorized
from the distraction of bees,
the song of yellow,
the eiyah   eiyah   eieiei   more rhythmic
                    than the Jesus prayer, insistent
as the endless murmuring of the knee-bending name.
Love mutterings to the sun, to Aton
Aton   Aton   to Aton, the Sun, to Re, the sunflowers
are singing to the sun, in all its known names, and to the erupting
    ends
of magnetic vortices on the sun's surface;
and these, the helium winds, fire throats, tenor back
            Promethean solos of power, are singing to the pointless
ones, anchoresses of the garden, earth's Poor Clares, contemplatives,
are singing to them, woman acolytes of the sun
who plead for the sun-wanting world,
singing to them,
keepers of the sacred instrument of pollen
who have willed all ego lightward
in a single, yellow, unblinking look,
singing, the sun singing to them, through them
Pax Mundi to the shivering world,
ataxic with its ferocious, blood-burst hallucinations,
the assurance of a meager good.

Pumpkins

Oompah   Oompah   Oompah, fattening
on the stem, tuba girthed, puffing like perorating parliamentarians,
Boompa   Boompah   Boompah,
earth hogs slurping swill from the sun,
jowels burp fat with photons, bigger, bigger, garden elephants,
mirthed like St. Francis, dancing (thud), dancing (thud,
brümpht, thud, brümpht) with the Buddha-bellied sun,
dolphin sweet, theatrical as suburban
children, yahooing a yellow
which whallops air. Pure. They are Socratically
ugly, God's jokes. O jongleurs, O belly laughs
quaking the matted patch, O my blimpish Prussian
generals, O garden sausages, golden zeppelins. How do? How do?
    How do?

Doo dee doo dee doooo.
What a rabble, some explode,
or sing, in the panic of September
sun, idiot praise for the sun that burns like a grand hotel,
for the sun, monstrous pulp in a groaning rind, flame seeded.
Popeyes, my dears, muscular fruit,
apoplexies of grunted energy flexed from the forearm vine,
self-hefted on the hill and shot
putted in the half-acre.

Carro-caroo.   Are you well,
my sweets, pleasure things, my baubles, my Poohs,
well?
I, weeding farmer, I, Caruso
them at dawn crow in the sun
cymballing mornings
and they Brunhilde back, foghorns, bloated alto notes

baroquely happy.
Not hoe teeth, not Rhotenone, but love,
bruited, busied, blessed these being-ward, barn-big,
bibulous on light, rampantly stolid
as Plato's Ideas, Easter Island
flesh lumps of meaning, rolling heads
in my 6-year-old nightmares,
vegetables on a ball and chain, sun anvils
booming with blows of temperature.

Come, phenomena, gourds of light, teach
your joy Esperanto, your intense Archimedean aha
of yellow to me, dung-booted serf, whose unhoed brain,
the garden's brightest fruit, ones
communion with the cowfaced cauliflowers,
cucumbers twinkling like toes, and you,
clown prince,
sun dauphin of the rioting plot.

Daphne Marlatt

small print

i

how little the reach, what is *love* love? its
impossible repeat attenuated through telephone
wire the light letter language of 'fax it,' hearts
darling and x's intend body's imprint, stand in for
the unremitting smell of your skin just there at
neck's bony hollow in your hair both kinds that
arc the pelvic ridge keys your other speech
close up and swollen lips aflare with wet
declaration *bold face*—without which i sleep
small print in the white of the page

ii

print small print it small enough not
to reach all of what love says when it
reads small in the whole of the page

iii

reading your voice attentive to solitude a
transient space love infiltrates anticipates
the feel of your skin its smell no word (nearness
then) resplendent breasting under the covers a
breathing space the city occludes its neon news
your voice removed my body walks its carbon
copy of yours deep in the bone

iv

not ready for you to say not ready print
not love printout plain as day not
ready you say for me to come home

v

to reach those little loves the pain of hills
animal words love-stark, enter in white a
void of cross-hatching covering distance unknown
intent scrawls xmas drift along the creek i follow
your declarative slant as you ascend out of the
limits of love a joy you wished language written
in quick gesture bold stride new reference i
try to decipher

vi

last call (it) how fast we unravel
love calls us i recall it
beside ourselves

vii

it's hearts darling attentive through tension to
the wire that closes round them stripping each
remark that separates familiar connection future
version sprung as nearness cuts with a ping the
words impossible and audible attachment taut to
the breaking point's heart strung

viii

love won't compute can't connect
words with what's felt, the fragile
murmur of memory fade, Y *save?*

ix

these small paraphs we sign trying the hours to
separate what's yours from mine, stand-in for
tongue's unremitted (f)lick keying the whole body
now no longer sent dot matrix gone to cruise two
truths *u* and *i* resolve out through, shaky vowels
looking for consonance where static interrupts
a clutch of mismatched lines. stop. no line at

x

repeat it small repeat all of
what love calls us back to

xi

night's byline grief enters quick mis/
take halfasleep makes the weight of the cat
curled in my groin your curve my hollow intimates
instant line of hip hand follows through on
empty, *you your* erased from day's vocabulary

xii

turned out of the inmost
intimate, cord between

    /cut/

your body and the word

xiii

leaves with this scrawl all of it unread
silence cannot cure septic override snow's late
light intensifies abstraction now skin's kinetics
fade i'm left disfiguring you

breakup inters trust
the dream *we*
entered in

imagination's scrap

Don McKay

Waking At The Mouth Of The Willow River

Sleep, my favourite flannel shirt, wears thin, and shreds, and birdsong happens in the holes. In thirty seconds the naming of species will begin. As it folds into the stewed latin of afterdream each song makes a tiny whirlpool. One of them, zoozeezoozoozee, seems to be making fun of sleep with snores stolen from comic books. Another hangs its teardrop high in the mind, and melts: it was, after all, only narrowed air, although it punctuated something unheard, perfectly. And what sort of noise would the mind make, if it could, here at the brink? Scritch, scritch. A claw, a nib, a beak, worrying its surface. As though, for one second, it could let the world leak back to the world. Weep.

Early Instruments

The wolf at the door
and the wolf in the forest and the work
work work of art. The scrape,
the chop, the saw tooth
tasting maple. The cradle, the cup, the muscle
in your mother's arm and back
and pelvis, muscle flexing in the air
between two people arguing,
two people loving, muscle
pumping blood. Gut
summoned to speak. The rotary cuff, the wrist,
having learnt the trick of witching wands and locks,
the heft, the grain, the web,
the rub of moving parts.
And the tiny sea in the ear
and the moth wing in the mind, which wait.

Chickadee Encounter

ok ok ok ok
here they come, the tidbits, the uppers,
animating the bramble,
whetting details. Hi,
I always say, I may be glum or dozy, still
hi, how's it going, every time they zip—
drawing that crisp invisible lilt from point to point—up
to check me out: ok: it's practically pauseless,
but as though some big machine—
domestication maybe—hiccupped,
a glitch through which the oceanic
thirsts of poetry pour: o
zippers, quicklings,
may you inherit earth, may you
perch at the edge of the shipwreck of state,
on the scragged uneconomical alders,
and chat.

The Laugh

"The inverse of language is like a laughter that
seeks to destroy language, a laughter infinitely
reverberated."
        —Emmanuel Levinas

The laugh that ate the snake and
runs through the city dressed in a sneeze, the mischief
done in these sly
passages of time, when the tongue is
severed from the voice and
fed to the weather, when the running
patter of catbirds simply
swallows the agenda, nothing to be held back,
nothing rescued in a catch-phrase or figure, your
house is on fire
and your children are gone.
When evenings pass as unseen
immaculate ships, and folk—
everyone is suddenly folk—rush to their porches
and lift their faces to this
effervescence of air,
wishing.
    Wishing what?
Just wishing.

Setting The Table

Knife

who comes to the table fresh
from killing the pig, edge
of edges,
entry into zip.
                    Knife
who can swim as its secret
through the dialogue or glimmer
in a kitchen drawer. Who first appeared
in God's hand to divide
the day from the night, then the sheep
from the goats, then from the other
sheep, then from their comfortable
fleeces. Nothing sinister in this except
it had to happen and it was the first
to have to. The imperative
mood. For what we are about to take
we must be grateful.

Fork

a touch of kestrel,
of Chopin, your hand with its fork
hovers above the plate, or punctuates
a proposition. This is the devil's favourite
instrument, the fourfold
family of prongs: Hard Place,
Rock, Something You Should Know,
and For Your Own Good. At rest,

face up, it says,
please, its tines
pathetic as an old man's fingers on a bed.
Face down it says
anything that moves.

Spoon

whose eloquence
is tongueless, witless, fingerless,
an absent egg.
Hi Ho, sing knife and fork, as off they go,
chummy as good cop and bad cop,
to interrogate the supper. Spoon waits
and reflects your expression,
inverted, in its tarnished moonlight. It knows
what it knows. It knows hunger
from the inside
out.

Sometimes A Voice (1)

Sometimes a voice—have you heard this?—
wants not to be voice any longer, wants something
whispering between the words, some
rumour of its former life. Sometimes, even
in the midst of making sense or conversation, it will
hearken back to breath, or even farther,
to the wind, and recognize itself
as troubled air, a flight path still
looking for its bird.
                I'm thinking of us up there
shingling the boathouse roof. That job is all
off balance—squat, hammer, body skewed
against the incline, heft the bundle,
daub the tar, squat. Talking,
as we always talked, about not living
past the age of thirty with its
labyrinthine perils: getting hooked,
steady job, kids, business suit. Fuck that. The roof
sloped upward like a take-off ramp
waiting for Evel Knievel, pointing into open sky. Beyond it
twenty feet or so of concrete wharf before
the blue-black water of the lake. Danny said
that he could make it, easy. We said
never. He said case of beer, put up
or shut up. We said
asshole. Frank said first he should go get our beer
because he wasn't going to get it paralysed or dead.
Everybody got up, taking this excuse
to stretch and smoke and pace the roof
from eaves to peak, discussing gravity
and Steve McQueen, who never used a stunt man, Danny's
life expectancy, and whether that should be a case

of Export or O'Keefe's. We knew what this was—
ongoing argument to fray
the tedium of work akin to filter vs. plain,
stick shift vs. automatic, condom vs.
pulling out in time. We flicked our butts toward the lake
and got back to the job. And then, amid the squat,
hammer, heft, no one saw him go. Suddenly he
wasn't there, just his boots
with his hammer stuck inside one like a heavy-headed
flower. Back then it was bizarre that,
after all that banter, he should be so silent,
so inward with it just to
run off into sky. Later I thought,
cool. Still later I think it makes sense his voice should
sink back into breath and breath
devote itself to taking in whatever air
might have to say on that short flight between the roof
and the rest of his natural life.

Kinds Of Blue #41 (Far Hills)

Viola, cello, double bass, the distances
deepen and address us. What is this language
we have almost learnt, or nearly not
forgotten, with its soft
introspective consonants, its drone
of puréed names? It says we ought to mourn
but not to grieve, it says that even loss
may be a place, it says
repose. The eye would like to fold its rainbow
like a fan, and quit
discriminating between this and that,
and indigo and mauve,
and go there. Once,
while sleeping in my down-filled sleeping bag
I dreamt of Eiders, diving
and diving into the dark Arctic Ocean, and
woke
bereft and happy, my whole mind
applauding.

Erin Mouré/Eirin Moure

Morphine, Or The Cutting Stone

A word is identical with a word & nothing else in the world
matches.

Outside the maples are manufacturing 30 feet of light. Snow
    tangles the air.
The ax is near the stone where wood has been split for years,
this stone, I could say, left by glaciers.
The house wall behind me.

I am alone here. Flutter. Your fires.

VARIIOUS INTRUSIONS

All of these cattle had leaked out of the body.

Herded up the road by men in yellow flowers.

The earth-moving equipment I was carrying on my shoulder
for this very purpose,
to shed the rain

One of the body's embarrassments

You pushing sudden your hand
(or I dreamed this, no
wanted)

A false consequence leads/ to another action.
The physical resemblance of the hand/ to any other hand, oh species.
To clarify this.

VARIIIOUS INTRUSIONNS

Trying to breed insolence into the body
The courage to sit up & bolt down the hospital corridor
gripping the IV bottle, the plastic lung hovering on the pole
glucose
water

Put my purse in that drawer, the patient said
When I hear the hiss, I know the morphine is coming
& I want my purse in that drawer

Don't touch my purse!

the small z under c
the caudillo (baf) of Spain raising his hand up, the suit he wore
of the army
His triumphant mouth open

The drawers painted white or ivory

SPECKLED CATTLE

All night the speckled cattle snort the seed out of the ground
or gourd,
not even waiting for the germination.

Why does the brain trigger a jumble-word
next to the real?
So you can't find the real word.
Gourd, you wake up, saying.
She is asleep beside you & does not hear this.

Quietly you go out to get water.
The pads on the little feet.
The claustrophobic smell of sleep

Snow falling outside on the ax-stone.
(Where the "n" went)

IMMENSE STRUCTURES

The poem is certainly an immense structure. Parts of it
you haven't see yet can make you shudder.

Light strung up under the open hood of the car, all that
greasy stuff in it, someone working on the motor
maybe your father

The light bounding off the garage wall, the immense
shadow, lines of light
bent stark against the tools.

Looking up at the grain of the plywood used for those walls,
unfinished, no gyproc ever added.
A light trip to the stars with astronauts.

Who "could" or "could not" be an astronaut (an argument).
An engineer, building civic bridges
over the Bow River.

It only makes sense, they said to her, you're a girl, you
can't be an astronaut. Listen to Mr. Krupa, darling,
you can't be an engineer either.

VARIIIIOUS INTRUSIONNS

Oh, Amelia, she sang, break my heart,
you don't have any right to appear in poetry.

Standing in your fab jeans & jacket beside the plane's wheel,
beside the postcard of Federico.

This could be a sonnet, this could be memorable.

FIELD COWS

Against the green field or white, the black & white cows
are speckled dreams we wake up to.
This could be a song by Sweat Voodoo, or could just be
a dream,
the snow gradually filling up the field, the south side of trees.
The cows are in their hot barn, getting hotter.
This could be a dream by Ajax Rising, this could be a dream by
Jerry Jerry, this could be a poem by Tepid Szlwyk, no,
stupid, this is feminist,
this could not be a poem by Mr. Szlwyk.

VARIOUS INTRUSIONSS

On the road with yellow cowboys, opening the fence wire,
the speckled rain falling on the dirt, making
slick oil,
sliding all over this road in the rented Oldsmobile.

God save us from the imperial slaughter, the
cabinet ministers mouthing an oath of office,

in the Chateau Imperial.

Tears have been shed otherwise for so much,
& here the cattle are walking on the roadside neither
black nor white but brown Herefords,
pale Charolais under the trees, spruce trees,
their specked skins so pretty, the fine hairs & bone structure,

the cowboys bowed before them in their yellow slickers,
reverent, the cows

hot from chewing
pine leaves, rhubarb, grasses, coal.

VAARIOUS INTRUSIONS

Oh, flutter. The snow clinging to the side of grasses,
good grasses, the cows literally *moving fields* of warmth,
steam from their nostrils

manufacturing next year's rain in the far mountains.
Ropes & slickers visible, yellow slickers & rain
running off the hat brim behind the cowboy's body,
the man's body,

opening the fence up to let the cattle pass.

An Oldsmobile on the cattle gate rattles like a cheap
xylophone, I was there, it is
Lived experience.

Their mouths open in the Imperial Hotel.
What about the Han Kings, she asks.

THE IMPERIAL HOTEL

The poem is encrusted with detritus already, making
the structure weighty, useless.
The patient is at home with the large-boned nurse,
making of dying a practical physiology, a job, a career emblem.

Here it is morning, I have the sheep jacket on
In my life once, I turned back from the green nightmare
Now outside the snow stilleth all things,*

I am going out to the cutting stone.

In memory of Bernie's friend Margaret

---

* & lifteth wonder unto the heart

from Sheep's Vigil for a Fervent Person

a *translation from the Portuguese of*
Alberto Caeiro's/Fernando Pessoa's O Guardador de Rebanhos

II *My sight's sharp as a sunflower*

My sight's sharp as a sunflower.
I walk up Winnett to Vaughn Road all the time
Looking left and right
And sometimes over my shoulder...
And what I see every moment
Is what no one's seen before me,
And, as such, I just let myself go...
I feel like a child in a T-shirt
Amazed by just being born
and realizing "hey, I'm born"...
I feel myself born at every moment
Into the World's eternity of the New...

I believe in the world and in marigolds,
Because I see them. But I don't think on it
For thinking can't understand...
The world isn't made for us to think in
(thinking is eye-sore)
But to gaze at, and to harken...

I've no philosophy: I've feelings...
I don't talk of Nature knowing what it is,
But just because I love it, and I love it "as such,"
For a lover never knows that which she loves
nor why, nor what love is...

To love is to abide in innocence,
hey, I'm still amazed . . .
And I'm 45, just pulling my t-shirt on . . .

XIV *Rhymes get on my nerves, Rarely*

I've got nothing to do with rhymes. Rarely
Are two trees equal, one beside the other.
"I think and write," and "flowers have colours"—
what do you think of those two trees rhymes?
I know my way of speaking isn't perfect
For I'm not what I appear to be
No, that would be too simple, too much like divinity.

I see and am heartened,
heartened like water runs out of a house with a crooked floor,
and my poetry is natural, like the wind picking up paper.

XVIII *What I'd give to be the sidewalk on Winnett*

What I'd give to be the sidewalk on Winnett
So that people without cars could trudge over me . . .

What I'd give to be the creek under the road at No Frills
So that people could sense water on the way to the laundromat

What I'd give to be the scrub poplars at the parking lot of No Frills
For they've just sky above and water below them

Well, and an ugly parking lot ...

What I'd give for a job at the mall, then just to sit on my ass
So they'd berate me for being slow, but admire my stamina ...

All this I'd rather, than pass through my life
Looking back, with such heartache, *desfeita* ...

XX *The Humber is pretty fabulous, really*

The Humber is more fabulous than the creek under my avenue.
And the Humber is no more fab than the creek under my avenue.
You can't mix up the two when on my avenue;
For that matter neither of them are very big ...

The Humber is too small for ships
Yet on its waters they still ply
For those who see the "not there" in all things:
The memory of canoes.

The Humber descends from up north
And the Humber enters Lake Ontario.
You always hear people say this on buses in the afternoon.
But few know the creek that races under Winnett

And where it heads
And where it came from.
And, as such, because fewer people claim it,
The creek of my avenue is more grand and free.

You can take the Humber out almost to Niagara Falls;
Beyond the Humber is America
Where fortunes are made.
No one ever thinks about what's beyond
the creek under Winnett Aveue.

The creek under my avenue makes no one think of anything.
Whoever goes to the edge of it has only reached the curb.

bp Nichol

Easter Pome

```
        pulpit           tulips
      pul    pit       tul    ips
    pu  l    p  it   tu  l    i  ps
   p  ul    p  i tt  u  l    i  p  s
   p  ul    p  t iu  t  l    i  p  s
   p  ul    t  u pl  i  t    i  p  s
   p  u t   u  l li  p  i    t  p  s
   p  t u   l  i up  l  p    i  t  s
    t  u l   i  p ps u  l    p  i  t
    t  u l   i  p sp u  l    p  i  t
     tu  l   i  ps    pu  l    p  it
      tul    ips       pul    pit
        tulips           pulpit
```

Cycle #22

```
drum   anda   wheel
anda   drum   andaw
heel   anda   druma
ndaw   heel   andad
ruma   ndaw   heela
ndad   ruma   ndawh
eela   ndad   ruman
dawh   eela   ndadr
uman   dawh   eelan
dadr   uman   dawhe
elan   dadr   umand
awhe   elan   dadru
mand   awhe   eland
adru   mand   awhee
land   adru   manda
whee   land   adrum
anda   whee   landa
drum   anda   wheel
```

landscape: 1

for thomas a. clark

alongthehorizongrewanunbrokenlineoftrees

song for saint ein

i look at you this way

noun then verb

these are my words

i sing to you

~

no separation no

the same thing

i am these words
these words say so

somewhere i exist separate from this page
this cage of sounds & signs

i am this noise

my voice says so

From Catullus Poem LI

Ill am I, paralyzed, whom God did hurt.
ill, suffering, a rare meal for gods
who sit, idle & adverse,
    watching & listening.

sweet ridicule, misery that ominous
spirits sense as meat, now, too simply,
Lesbia, that pixie, eats me for supper
    with her golden voice.

language speaks its torture, tenous sub-articulations
inflame my madness, sonnets of supplicants
tinkle in the air, gem-like talking to
    light my darkness.

Opium—Catullus: to be is to be molested
open & exultant in my numb genesis:
opium & rage pry & beat at
    my fading sight.

love song 2

just once to say 'i love you' all the feeling felt
to dwell inside the words as they are spoken
(not broken on the tongue by my intent
conscious or otherwise
to hold back in speech each feeling
behind the syntax of my own attention
naming song what never sings
but is a circling in my tension round you)
that desire to 'say' totally
in gesture as in word
all that i do feel for you
locked up in hesitations i give you as poems

a little song

for george bowering

a
blake
lake

keats
eats

shelley
hell
he

et
rossetti

Michael Ondaatje

The Nine Sentiments

(Historical Illustrations on Rock and Book and Leaf)

i

All day desire
enters the hearts of men

Women from the village of _____
move along porches
wearing calling bells

Breath from the mouth
of that moon

Arrows of flint
in their hair

ii

She stands in the last daylight
of the bedroom painting her eye,
holding a small mirror

The brush of sandalwood along the collarbone

Green dark silk

A shoe left
on the cadju tree terrace

these nights when "pools are
reduced by constant plungings"

Meanwhile a man's burning heart
his palate completely dry
on the Galapitigala Road

thinking there is water in that forest

    iii

Sidelong coquetry
at the Colombo Apothecary

Desire in sunlight

Aliganaya—"the embrace
during an intoxicated walk"
or "sudden arousal
while driving over speed bumps"

Kissing the birthmark
on a breast,
tugging his lotus stalk
(the literal translation)
on Edith Grove

Or "conquered on a car seat"
along Amarasekera Mawatha

One sees these fires
from a higher place
on the cadju terrace

they wander like gold
ragas of longing
like lit sequin
on her shifting green dress

iv

States of confusion as a result
of the movement of your arm
or your hidden grin

The king's elephants
have left for war
crossing the rivers

His guards loiter in the dark corridors
full of chirping insects

My path to this meeting
was lit by lightning

Your laughter with its
intake of breath. *Uhh huh.*

Kadamba branches driven
by storm into the bedroom

Your powdered anus
your hair on my stomach
releasing its heavy arrow

        v

The curve of the bridge
against her foot

her thin shadow falling
through slats
into water movement

A woman and her echo

The kessara blossom she kicks
in passing that flowers

You stare into the mirror
that held her painted eye

Ancient dutiful ants
hiding in the ceremonial
yak-tail fan
move towards and climb
her bone of ankle

The Bhramarah bee is drunk
from the south pasture

this insect that has
the letter "r" twice
in its name

    vi

Five poems without mentioning the river prawn.

    vii

The women of Boralesgamuwa
uproot lotus in mid-river
skin reddened by floating pollen

Songs to celebrate the washing
of arms and bangles

This laughter when husbands are away

An uncaught prawn hiding by their feet

The three folds on their stomachs
considered a sign of beauty

They try out all their ankle bracelets
during these afternoons

    viii

The pepper vine shaken and shaken
like someone in love

Leaf patterns

saffron and panic seed
on the lower pillows
where their breath met

while she loosened
from her hips the string
with three calling bells

her fearless heart
light as a barn owl
against him all night

ix

An old book on the poisons
of madness, a map
of forest monasteries,
a chronicle brought across
the sea in Sanskrit slokas.
I hold all these
but you have become
a ghost for me.

I hold only your shadow
since those days I drove
your nature away.

A falcon who became a coward.

I hold you the way astronomers
draw constellations for each other
in the markets of wisdom

placing shells
on a dark blanket
saying "these
are the heavens"

calculating the movement
of the great stars

x

Walking through rainstorms to a tryst,
the wet darkness of her aureoles

the Sloka, the Pada, the secret Rasas

the curved line of her shadow

the Vasanta-Tilaka or Upajati metres

bare feet down ironwood stairs

A confluence now
of her eyes,
her fingers, her teeth
as she tightens the hood
over the gaze of a falcon

Love arrives and dies in all disguises
and we fear to move
because of old darknesses
or childhood danger

So our withdrawing words
our skating hearts

xi

Life before desire,
without conscience.
Cities without rivers or bells.

Where is the forest
not cut down
for profit or literature

whose blossoms instead
will close the heart

Where is the suitor
undistressed
one can talk with

Where is there a room
without the damn god of love?

Lisa Robertson

Residence At C_____

Give me hackneyed words because
they are good. Brocade me the whole body
of terrestrial air. Say spongy ground
with its soft weeds. Say self because it can.
Say arts of happiness. Say you have died.
Say sequin because the word just
appeared. Say weather take this adult
from its box. Memorize being sequined
to something, water. Everything you forget
inserts love into the silent money.
Memorize huge things of girders greased. Say
the water parting about the particular
animal. Say what happens to the face
as it gala tints my simple cut
vicious this afternoon the beautiful
light on the cash is human to guzzle
with—go away wild feelings, there you go
as the robin as the songsparrow go
the system shines with uninterrupted
light. It's petal caked. Leaves shoot up. Each
leaf's a runnel. Far into the night a
sweetness. Marvelous. Spectacular. Brilliant.
Clouded towards the south. It translates
Lucretius. Say cup of your heart rush
sluice is yellow sluice Kate Moss is Rousseau
have my arms. Say impasto of
atmosphere for her fur. Halo open
her face. Misplace the death. All the truth
under the tree has two pinky oozy

names. Say trying to possess or not. Say
if you thought love was ironical. If
pleasure emancipates, why aren't you some-
where. Sincerity.

Tuesday

Days heap upon us. All plain. All clouds except a narrow opening at the top of the sky. All cloudy except a narrow opening at the bottom of the sky with others smaller. All cloudy except a narrow opening at the bottom of the sky. All cloudy except a narrow opening at the top of the sky. All cloudy. All cloudy. All cloudy. Except one large opening with others smaller. And once in the clouds. Days heap upon us. Where is our anger. And the shades darker than the plain part and darker at the top than the bottom. But darker at bottom than top. Days heap upon us. Where is Ti-Grace. But darker at the bottom than the top. Days heap upon us. Where is Christine. Broken on the word culture. But darker at the bottom than the top. Days heap upon us. Where is Valerie. Pulling the hard air into her lung. The life crumbles open. But darker at the bottom than the top. Days heap upon us. Where is Patty. Unlearning each thing. Red sky crumbles open. This is the only way to expand the heart. But darker at the top than the bottom. Days heap upon us. Where is Shulamith. Abolishing the word love. The radical wing crumbles open. The scorn is not anticipated. We have given our surface. Darker at the top than the bottom. Except one large opening with others smaller. Except one large opening with others smaller. Gradually. Days heap upon us. Where is Patricia. In the dream of obedience and authority. The genitalia crumble open. It is only ever a flickering. We never worshipped grief. It has been stuccoed over. Half cloud half plain. Half cloud half plain. Half plain. One in the plain part and one in the clouds. Days heap upon us. Where is Jane. Looking for food. Hunger crumbles open. All this is built on her loveliness. We have fallen into a category. Love subsidized our descent. Streaky clouds at the bottom of the sky. Days heap upon us. Where is Mary. In the extreme brevity of the history of parity. Rage crumbles open. It felt like dense fog. What is fact is not necessarily human. Memory anticipiates. Authority flows into us like a gel. We cross the border to confront the ideal. Streaky cloudy at the top of the sky. Days heap upon us. Where is Grace. Spent in sadness. The underground crumbles open. There is no transgression possible. We publicly mobilize the horror of our emotion. It is a phalanx. The clouds darker than the plain or blue part and darker at the top than the bottom. Days heap upon us. Where is Gloria. Pushing down laughter. Utopia crumbles open. It is an emotion similar to animals sporting. We won't plagiarize shame. Like this we solve herself. The clouds darker than the plain part and darker at the top than the bottom. The clouds darker than the plain part and darker at the top than the bottom. The clouds lighter than the plain part and darker at the top than the bottom. The clouds lighter than the plain part and darker at the bottom than top. The clouds lighter than the plain part and darker at the top than the bottom. The lights of the clouds lighter and the darks darker than the plain part and darker at the top than the bottom. The same as the last but darker at the bottom than the top. The same as the last but darker at the bottom than the top. Days heap upon us. Where is Violette. Walking without flinching. Doubt crumbles open. It is not a value but a disappearance. We come upon the city in our body. The same as the last. The same as the last. The same as the last. The tint once over in the plain part, and twice in the clouds. Days heap upon us. Where is Emily. Out in all weather. Dignity crumbles open. There is not even a utopia. We would have to mention all the possible causes of her death. The tint once over the openings and twice in the clouds. Days heap upon us. Where is Olympe. Going without rest. The polis crumbles open. This is no different than slow war. The tint twice in the openings and once in the clouds. Days heap upon us. Where is Michelle. Homesick for anger. Midnight crumbles open. The tint twice in the openings. The tint twice over. Days heap upon us. Where is Bernadine. At description. The tint twice over. Days heap upon us. Where is Kathleen. The tint twice. The clouds darker than the plain part and darker at the top than the bottom. The clouds lighter than the plain part and darker at the top than the bottom. The lights of the clouds lighter. The others smaller. The same as the last. The same as the last. The tint twice in the openings and once in the clouds. Days heap upon us. The tint twice over. Days heap upon us. With others smaller. With others smaller.

Residence At C_____

My purpose here is to advance into
the sense of the weather, the lesson of
the weather. Forever I'm the age 37
to calm my mind. I'm writing sentences here
of an unborrowed kind. The sky is
mauve lucite. The light lies intact and
folded. You can anticipate the wind.
A slight cloud drifts contrary to the
planet. Everything I'm writing about
begins as the robin as the song
sparrow begins is description
animals are description sparkling
scrapping in loose shrieks teenagers also
utopia is memory the broken
bits running motors leaves remarkably
simple and heart shaped and practical
as leaves the gentlest flavour of them is
description and islands of written
stuff love operas and suicides vast
itineraries of error, memory
grey silk sky with pigeons circling
description because memory can't
love as the orange lights of description
beneath the birds which appear to be strings
of memory in speaking of this small
thing, repeatedly to speak of some small
proximity and in what ways the tough
days pass into languor smoke trees brightgrey
clouds moving in Heaven, streets with
clouds or dripping mist, the mist touching the
golden age of untranslatability, no
distinction: just the fear of isolation

from objects and from the clouds, breathing
arguments I wish to touch as
if the touch were emblem of the scene of novelty.
'Tis not my purpose to retrace the under-
thirst, then the severance. I'll finger
sincerity, by exemplum relate
a portrait of my luck.

Anne Simpson

Seven Paintings By Brueghel

The Triumph Of Death

These watches. Ticking, still. Each hour is cold:
the rims surround quick voices. Shut in rooms.
Gone. *Tick*. The towers. *Tock*. Of fire. A fold
in air. We're smoke, drifting. A painted doom
where cities burn and ships go down. Death's
dark sky—a grainy docudrama. Time
swings bones on circus wheels. Listen: wind's breath,
a shriek. *Theatrum Mundi*. In their prime,
the living. Leapt. That buckling of the knees.
Then gunshots: plastic bags on fences. Snapping.
Or loose. *Thank you—shop—at*. The lovers see
nothing. He plays a lute. She sings. Clapping—
machines sift through debris for the remains.
A sales receipt, a shoe. The silvery rain.

Landscape With The Parable Of The Sower

A sales receipt, a shoe. The silvery rain
has many hands. A stream—Fresh Kills—elides
with river. Thick and slow. A landfill plain:
a ghost in biohazard gear. Gulls ride
the thermals, circling high as barges come,
a linking chain. Blue metropolis, far-
off glints of light. The cranes all lift and hum,
making hills of metal, bone. Crushed cars.
So garbage rises: this stench is monument.
Yet Brueghel's farmer takes the seeds, flings wide
his arm. A miracle: small event. We meant
to go, but every boat was laden. Tides
pulled home, pulled here, then left us for the birds.
We take the shape of soil, abandon words.

The Tower Of Babel I

We take the shape of soil, abandon words.
The world will change without us. Did we glean
a little shine? Perhaps. These wheeling birds
drift down to earth. Crying. The air, unseen,
seeks entry without keys. All locked, shut down.
A spackled light gets through. We merely craved
a taste. *Hello, my name is* _____. A crown,
a king. One makes the other into slave.
Behind is Babel's core. Red as a heart
opened for bypass. Laid bare. Wind, idling.
It's quiet. Still. The horses, loaded carts,
are stuck. The ships, the docks. Thin bridles
of cloud. All stopped. Each thing unclocked, undone.
A man who kneels to plead his case. Warm sun.

The Tower Of Babel II

That man who knelt to plead his case, that sun:
they're gone. In time, air hardens, growing dark.
The wars go on; beyond the TV, guns
talk to themselves. One, two. They whisper, bark.
Erotica. And Babel: height's desire
is weary of itself, but there's no end
to greed. A cruise, a condo. Guests for hire.
On the rug: a shirt, a shoe. Whatever bends
one body to another. We've forgotten.
Those painted clouds are knives. Slipped in walls
between the ribs. This plot device: rotten —
the thing exploded from within. Small
papers, white flakes. Last wish. Someone's cellphone.
("Are you still there? *Are you*?") A voice falls. Stone.

The Slaughter Of The Innocents

"Are you still there? *Are you*?" A voice falls. Stone,
unbearable stone. It grinds. It tastes of grief.
Don't watch. Go blind. Oh Lord, those moans
will haunt us. This one. That one there. Brief
lives. Snow. And here, between the black trees, blood.
A leaping dog. A bird. Everywhere we turn
there's whiteness in the air. And memory, a flood
of killings no kindness can assuage. Urns
half-full of ashes: nothing that we knew
of those we loved. So young. Such shining hair,
those gleams recalled. A silence follows through
the rooms of when and how. Now, up the stairs
a rescuer is climbing. But he's too late.
And look what happened. This. Short straw of fate.

Hunters In The Snow

Who knows what happened? A short straw of fate,
all that. Years ago. But now we've changed;
those terrors tucked back in the heart. "Just great,
that weekend special: everything arranged."
We return; the house looks strange. Each thing
deceives. The counters, cutlery. Believe
the chairs; they guard the table in a ring.
The hunters come. They're trudging, slow. Reprieve
makes curving flight, a song in evening's sky:
pale green at dusk. Some children skate; they laugh.
And history has no place. Easy to lie
on queen-sized beds, *dream a little dream*. Half-
heard, the phantoms speak: No, you weren't there—
We turn; we sleep. But once there was a prayer.

Christ And The Adulteress

We turn; we sleep. But once there was a prayer,
a way to finger mystery. It floats,
one plastic bag, freed from the fence, that snare
with loops of wire. We translate into motes,
a glimmer in a shaft of sun. One glide,
we're gone. A painted scene: against this plea
is set a stone. An end. Each thing is tried.
A man makes notes in sand. The wind goes free.
One gust: his words are ghosts. The dust, absolved,
has vanished too. First kiss, last glance. *Tick. Tock.*
All goes to ground. We kneel down and dissolve.
Turn in. Turn out of time. Where nothing's clocked.
A touch: so light. Love's breath. Things we can't hold:
these watches. Ticking. Still. Each hour is cold.

Karen Solie

Cardio Room, Young Women's Christian Association

You won't know me. Any resemblance
to the woman I was is purely
agricultural. That fluff. A pink annual
given to low-born intemperate acts
unbecoming a modern person. No more.
I'm tough. Nothing
could eat me. No profligate billy
with a hacking cough, or that old goat
and his yen for plagues, floods, and burning
fun places to the ground. Not you,
either. There was a time
I rolled like dough, plumped up
to be thumped down with artless yeasty
chemistry. Dumpling. Honeybun.
I sickened some. But evolved
in a flash, like the living flak
of a nuclear mistake. In space-age fabrics
I've moved more iron than a red
blood cell, climbing and climbing
the new world's dumbest tower. I'm on
to this. Alongside the rest
I sweat it out with the smug one-party
affability of a sport utility
vehicle. Deceptively little cargo space.
Even covered in mud I look great.

Meeting Walter Benjamin

A long lake in a swan-throated bed, longer
than wide by seventy miles. In his loneliness you mistake him
for shade creaking from the poplars, his gait that way,
eyes down, backlit, its yet-againness. He mistakes you in kind
for a snag of brome, for in your loneliness
you have forgotten the grammar of description—no,
the *why* of it—and become just another little bit
of what's there, unable as grass is to explain itself. Here,
above the mudline of a Saskatchewan valley, and he
has never seen one. When he speaks
it's from midpoint over the dog-hued water, his voice
thrown, a bond loosened and winging on the updraft
past your ear. It's real, he says,
your disappointment. Wind stirs up hill colour like a stick
in paint, Fauvist with hidden deer in this seed-heavy
fall among a wet year's curious late-bloomers, the air convex,
retinal. Follow his eye: *Angelus Novus* up against
the barbed wire, blown backward, disconsolate as anyone
with a grasp of history. You've read that grace
abides in a law of downward motion. He says despair
is in the details. Don't look,
he tells you. Then, look.

Thrasher

Yellow-legs ekes lower at nightfall to a stick nest
brambled in the shade-kill, doing for himself, deft

as a badger in a hammock. Mornings, toeing wracked heights
of the cottonwood, he flaps his brown flag above alkaline

slough beds, over plowlands attesting
to the back and forth of work, their brown degrees

scriven by road allowance cut at right angles through shriven
weeds, fenceposts bracketing brown rut lines slantwise

in relief. In relief at the topmost, he mimics domestic, migrant,
spaniel, spring peepers, quacks, urks, and gurgles akin

to a four-stroke in heavy water. He's slightly

off. None respond. His own call is the vinyl scratch
between tracks, a splice point. He was hatched

that way, ferruginous, a wet transistor
clacking from the egg in which he had lain curled

as an ear with an itch inside. He carries on
like AM radio. Like a prison rodeo. Recounts loser

baseball teams, jerry-riggers, part-timers, those paid in scrip,
anyone who has come out of retirement once

too often. He is playbacks, do-overs, repeats, repeats
the world's clamorous list, makes it his, replete,

and fledges from persistence what he is.

An Argument For Small Arms

The shock is that it took
so long, this trajectory played out
in a fizzle toward the words
I understand. By suppertime
on the first day of what's left, the stock
of a small bore .22 fits smartly
at the shoulder. Home,
home. Suppose this is it. Loaded.
Leveled. A rote stance
squared off to the fence
and the trash set up there. Empties.
Their cylindrical shadows lie
uneasily upon the ragweed. This
is the man-made moment. Extension
of the arm, the eye, the mind's
follow-through to an end
in shards. The clap and recoil
of continuity, cracked. Air torn
like a letter through the middle
of before and after.

Larking

What swimmers. We cannot leave lie
any excuse to pitch into the drink. Nights,
as our lifeguards sleep, but nooners too,
and tea time. A dip first thing will goose

the blood up. The grounded are a bore.
They toss inflatables out from shore,
trot home to call their friends: *yes*
old so-and-so's in headfirst again.

And we are buoyant for a spell. Until
sogged, we emerge heartbroken, skint,
or just made fool of, prone to fever or the itch,
and must dry out. Those landlocked stints

a rocky province, grimly lit
with no high ground to recommend it.

Emergency Response

You want love but not to give up anything
of your life, its situations—
whatever it is that you do. Never mind.
To hear this will bring no one any joy.
Something undoubtedly needs work. Surely
a knob has fallen off somewhere. The fixed
don't stay that way. It's a comfort,
actually, this perpetual loosening, the world
wearing on everything in it as when a taut hour
slackens into rain. Far greater for you
the consolation of repair, the glueing
and reglueing of various legs, all the snapped
handles. Raised by sandbaggers, you believe
in hammers and nails. Now that what you want
has tooled in on its wobbly wheels
you've hauled up like a journeyman
with a wrench in your hand. And love
standing by, nearly in uniform, waiting
for it all to come apart.

More Fun In The New World

I lied about the shortcut, the high road,
all of it. Steered through the same recreational districts
dry-eyed and frostbit, as if on rails, and pulled up
just like that. Eight yards to the motel office, one more
to ring the bell. The ice machine means well, a grey slab
I attend with my bucket. I've been here before,
paced it off and slept beneath a sheet
forty feet from the highway. Darling,
they're tearing up the highway. When I said so long
I meant that I don't understand modern manners or the solar system
or anything. That a crucial lesson
didn't take. The new math ruined a generation. Just look
what we count on: blink of binary
operations. On check-in I find hair in the drain, a ring
by the phone, as though I'm late. Too late. At check-out
I buy more time for the purpose of making suspiciously
little noise, unable to believe a mid-size Canadian airport
the last place I will ever see you. Come back. I'm low
on cash, downgrading, looking
at what poverty means to show me. This bed,
burned by cigarettes. The chair beside it.

Todd Swift

Homage To Charlotte Rampling

Not to be just a "skinny sado-masochist"
twisted past all recognition, suspenders
over fishbone torso and tweenie nipples
singing in the death camp to your lover:

that was, Charlotte, a wise career move.
So was the departure to alter ego Paris.
Marriage suited you better than nakedness
set in the most perverse circumstances

imaginable. Older, in *Under The Sand*,
Ozon's film, your eyes identify the body
of your drowned husband, no longer human
but swollen by the sea, putrid and sexless.

Your gaze lies over the available absence
we all tend to as volatile organic creatures.
The loss and horror and the contamination
under the white dry sheets in the mortuary,

pulled aside like the skin from a surgical
wound. Your eyes hover, they stay open.
We see you struggle, there, in that moment with
what we all have to face. Your face dies for us.

The Influence of Anxiety at the Seaside With Tea

She saw the beauty of the sea and could not rival it
For lack of depth, for cut and clarity. It screened
Itself like a blue movie. It was a mandolin. Flat,
And on a continuous feed. The sea was a pool

On a spool, a fluid, wet circuitry, a freakish
Cola, without sugar or fizz. The sea was in business
To sell waves to sand; to deliver cetaceans to nets;
The sea is a grey-green, moon-led elephant

Who always forgets. She sank into the Sargasso
Of herself, and touched a wreck. It yielded doubloons
And Maltese falcons and other encrusted valuables;
She scooped the ice-cream starfish and the jelly

Of the sperm whales, and the cardboard villainy
Of certain sharks. She slid like a shadow, a dagger
Of slim ease in a pressurised medium. She sang
Oxygen and filtered sunlight, and salty tunes.

She was overcome by *Harmonium,* poems flushed
With quince and tea and royal-rococo references
To the world and imagination; dove, in homage;
She wrapped herself in a peacock-daubed kimono

In silken envy. How could she not be immensely
Injured by the creations of Florida and San Juan?
The ocean and its sisters set out its store of baubles,
And she bought them. She was the eye and womb

Of the stanzas that melted and ran through the town
Like rough blue-white bulls storming a seawall.
This was the first performance of the storm, the horn
Section was off. The rain pulled toads from its hat.

The world was brushed with cream like a scone.
Happiness was inherited and could not be taxed.
She swam Olympic strokes, and sang circular tracks.
The sea undressed, a Parisian girl, *oh la la, mais oui.*

Leaving Paris

So now I bid farewell to my barber
Hugues Renaut, who I saw
For two years in Paris, every six weeks,
For *Coiffure & Soins*. This last

Of my times with him, Hugues sits
In his own chair, the one I was always in,
As his brother works his thinning skull.
He gazes into the mirror like a king

Whose crown has come off his head.
Then they switch places, twins at home
Sharing brush, comb, and scissors.
Although I promise to return long before

My black hair has reached my collar,
We both know the distances we won't
Cross to come across each other, again.
His usual banter pared down to slight lack,

I shake hands and step out into *rue d'Assas*.
The lady at the *Tabac* sold *Marlboro Lights*
And English papers to me. Nothing more.
But, after only a year or so, I loved her,

Even when she stood behind the counter
Beside her husband, a hulking man
With a Renaut-trimmed beard and no smile.
One of her hands was missing a finger.

The Tenant Of Wildfeld Hall

I miss being a kid, but barely recall those parts
About chores, not getting kissed, or being ugly.
And the palpability of novels. Opening
Helen's copy she lent that Sunday afternoon,
By Monday I was hooked, on gothic winds
And girls in cloaks, and love, for characters
That were actually her, or so I felt. Returning
The loan, she looked at me, as if I was already
Forgotten, but didn't bother to ask me not to stay.
Death's not about going to the block for a woman
Whose better husband you robustly replace.
Living is more like falling forward on your face,
Onto a scuffed parquet floor, lightly dusted
With all those who have been swept off it before.

Ballad Of The Solitary Diner

When I eat alone, I am alone.
Thank God I have my books.
Friends? Not many.
My wife, in her tower, earning money.
A few who live in other countries

Too far to go to share a meal.
When I sit down at noon I often feel
As sad as a man having married
The moon. You cannot love well
Someone you can't share a spoon

With, be it soup or salad.
The waiter or waitress assumes
The identity of a temporary friend,
But they are busy with their errands
And soon go to other people.

Then, as my tea cools, and the day
Gets weak in the head and fails
To keep appearances up,
I put on my winter coat to pay,
Leave a pound for their trouble,

And go out the way I came in.
Thank God I have my books.
I can tell by the limited smiles
As I turn, I no longer have my looks.
It is a shame we have to eat at all,

It hurts us to have to be so open
And quiet, even as we appear social.
If I could get by on my poetry
I'd eat a page a day in my flat.
I'd stay thin, and not become fat

As all this dining out in the world
Has made me: yes, and with nothing
To show for the tedious work
Of getting it down, but one more check
And a dark walk home, through a town.

Fred Wah

3 Pictograms From The Interior Of BC

Lost
amidst Caloplaca
and rising
as a bubble
from earth to sky

How does she know that
How does she do all that walking
through the forest
How does she know the bears won't get her?

jumped   over
the moon   the house   elk muskrat & beaver
all runs away   runs away
over & over
& over & over &

Father/Mother Haibun #4

Your pen wrote Chinese and your name in a smooth swoop
with flourish and style, I can hardly read my own tight
scrawl, could you write anything else, I know you could
read, nose in the air and lick your finger to turn the large
newspaper page pensively in the last seat of those half-
circle arborite counters in the Diamond Grill, your glass
case bulging your shirt pocket with that expensive pen,
always a favourite thing to handle the way you treated it
like jewellery, actually it was a matched pen and pencil set,
Shaeffer maybe (something to do with Calgary here), heavy,
silver, black, gold nib, the precision I wanted also in things,
that time I conned you into paying for a fountain pen I
had my eye on in Benwell's stationery store four dollars
and twenty cents Mom was mad but you understood such
desires in your cheeks relaxed when you worked signing
checks and doing the books in the back room of the cafe
late at night or how the pen worked perfectly with your
quick body as you'd flourish off a check during a busy
noon-hour rush the sun and noise of the town and the cafe
flashing.

**High muck-a-muck's gold-toothed clicks ink mark red green
on lottery blotting paper, 8-spot (click, click)**

Father/Mother Haibun #11

Mother somewhere you flying over me with love and close
careless caress from Sweden your soft smooth creme skin
only thoughts from your mother without comparison the
lightness of your life/blood womaness which is mine despite
language across foetalness what gods of northern europe
bring out of this sentence we say and live in outside of
the wife of the storm god's frictive battle with the 'story'
our names

Rain washes first snow, old words here on the notepad,
'Where did Odysseus go?'

Music At The Heart Of Thinking 22

ALWAYS THINK THINKING INSIDE MYSELF NO PLACE
without death Kwakiutl song sings or watch sit
scramble and catch last blue Pacific horizon no
end to the complete thought transference of
which the words "circling eyes" Mao knew this
is the life writing questions even every rock
etched in wonder sometimes that song feels like
the master paradigm or river we return to with
a sigh the archipelago syntagmed "empty from
breathing" but the body as a place that is as a
container has suddenness so the politics of
dancing is a dead giveaway to the poet's
"nothing will have taken place but the place."

Music At The Heart Of Thinking 42

Is that the flesh made word
or is that the flesh-made word?

Is that get it entirely right
or is that somewhat wrongly?

Le mot juste or just tomatoes?

The poem as a field of carrots or stones?

You, squinting, as I tell you.

Telling you, you telling me, field waiting.

Music At The Heart Of Thinking 52

tongue mist lip boat brown gull hill town bed
stone shadow crow tooth rain boat flood ham-
mer star grill shadow skin hammer mouth town
mist hill rock brown bed bird tongue snow creek
lip crow circle brown lip wave boat shadow city
light hill sky mouth talk snow gull hammer fog
moon wet grey stone boat bed mist skin gill
word flood crow tongue river mouth star brown
lip night flood sail wave sky tooth rock red bird
shadow stone snow city blue hammer bed hill
crow tongue

Music At The Heart Of Thinking 54

How numbers make trails.
Track LiPo to Castelgar,
the Kootenay River flows down from the sky,
never returns.

And chance to get it in the way
of water's predictability
or the white clouds of pacific
western mountain flesh.

Birth is like that, though.
Homes, mothers, names,
friends as images. Puffs
of imagic "rift or lake," anyplace.

Notation of these events quad right. He's got
                              ideas fixed.
Video la province, video la country, Winnipeg.

Hold it! When imprint hits grapheme
then eme is as in memory
                    just an echo.

Jan Zwicky

You Must Believe In Spring

Because it is the garden. What is left to us.
Because silence is not silence without sound.
Because you have let the cat out, and then in, and then out,
    and then in, and then out, and then in, and then
    out, and then in, and then out, and then in,
    enough.
Because otherwise their precision at the blue line would
    mean nothing.
Because otherwise death would mean nothing.
Because the light says so.
Because a human being can gladly eat only so much cabbage.
Because the pockets of your overcoat need mending.
Because it's easy not to.
Because your sweaters smell.
Because Gregory of Nazianzen said geometry has no place in
    mourning, by which he meant despair presumes too
    much.
Because it ain't over 'til it's over.—Hank Aaron, Jackie
    Robinson. Satchel Paige.
Because Kant was wrong, and Socrates, Descartes and all the
    rest. Because it is the body thinking and Newt
    Gingrich would like you not to.
Because the signs are not wrong: you are here.
Because I love you. Or you love someone. Because someone
    is loved.
Because under the sun, everything is new.
Because the wet snow in the trees is clotted light.
Because in 1841 it took six cords of wood to get through a
    winter in one room at Harvard and two-thirds
    of Maine used to be open country as a result.
Because sleeping is not death.
Because although an asshole was practising his Elvis Presley

imitation, full voice, Sunday morning, April 23rd
at Spectacle Lake Provincial Park, the winter wren
simply moved 200 yards down the trail.
Because the wren's voice is moss in sunlight, because it is
a stream in sunlight over stones.
Because Beethoven titled the sonata.
I mean: would Bill Evans *and* Frank Morgan lie to you?
Because even sorrow has a source.
For, though it cannot fly, the heart is an excellent clamberer.

Lilacs

Restless, I walk out in the evening
to the old house; to the patio around the back
where the old lilacs bloom.
This is a surprise, for I would have said
I do not like this place, would not
come to it by choice:
the peeling lattice on the south side,
the crumbling cinder blocks that once made
a failed sort of fireplace on the east.
The pad was small, but even so
you have to pick your feet up not to stumble
where the concrete cracked.

The lilacs lean across the south-east corner,
blocking the walk.
If you asked my sister, she would say
it never happened, but I remember that
one spring we tamed a bumble-bee
when it came in the afternoons to feed.
She denies this now, of course,
or would; refuses any salvage, claims I'm inventing
if I say there were moments when the sun came out
like her hair in the shadows of the leaves, heavy, like cream, cut
blunt as a spoon, her small teeth
as she laughed up at me, the bee
humming in my palm as she stroked it; and though I
think hope may be a better guide to the past than despair

I now doubt, too—these lilacs
are probably thick with insects in the afternoons, it's
ridiculous to think we might have sat inside them safe,
you'd have to be careful, merely brushing by,
not to be stung. When you think of it
she must be right, because why else
would she deny it, and I bury my face
as I might imagine leaning into sea-foam:
cool, explosive; the way her hand
when it touched me could unlock the bone under its skin,
or how the drowned must feel,
rising through themselves from the ocean floor.

Beethoven: Op. 95

Nel mezzo del cammin di nostra vita
mi retrovai per una selva oscura

I

An apology, first: I did not guess
the moodiness my middle years
would bring, unschooled as I was
in the varieties of frustration.
You were right: stupidity
surrounds us, and our own
splits the skull most sharply.
Also: that nothing
is achieved without the grimmest labour
on the slenderest of hopes
(except perhaps for Wolfgang, who was not
entirely human).
Not even music comes in its own words.

The importance of walks,
your duty to your nephew,
and the muscle in a true *cantabile*: you were right
about discipline, and politics,
the steep well of fury, and finally
what the fury goes through to: love
like a hand through the wall of the chest,
like a hand in fire, fire
tearing itself, in the hand's flame
a heart, in the heart's fist
an ear.

II

Remember this one?
Twenty-six miles he runs, in the sun,
Marathon to Athens, his heart
punching the blood through his lungs, runs
it will turn out—though he
won't live to know this—to announce
the dawning of the Golden Age.

The walls, and then the gate;
and the news that he has come
spreading before him like
the bright pool from a sacrifice, and still
he runs: to the agora,
to the Council Chamber, now
someone has recognized him and it's guessed
what news he brings; he slows—the crowd
behind him, shifting, tense—hauls
hugely on the air, roars *joy,*
we are victorious
and drops dead.

It's beside the point
the story is apocryphal. Myth is history
we need. And what matters is
the bit off camera,
not a goatherd or a guide car in sight,
around mile twenty, say, when the message
could be anything: the truth
has struck his body—*this*
cannot be done—but he takes

the next step anyway. Not out of loyalty
or pride, but because he is a runner,
and he wills it. And what matters is

some facts exhaust us this way, too.
We fight until the spirit's stripped,
nothing between us and the bare floor of the self, and then
the thing that cannot happen
happens, the thing that no one sees:
some place past emptiness
we take another step.

III

Hearing, you have reached the end,
the kernel bitter in your mouth.
Where would you go
even if your throat would open?
Only in the country,
relief (o, in the country!)—as if
every tree spoke.

If all comes to naught,
if all comes to naught...
All is coming to naught,
but the earth, sweet stillness,
remains, will remain. Woods,
hearing stillness, remain...

This plague, my hearing.
Only in the country, praise.
Only on the earth, sweetness.
Music, this sweetness,
deer in the twilight:
o hearing, o earth,
remain.

IV

A walk in autumn fields, the smell
of hay and dust not unlike
a canvas tent. In a year of downpours,
a week without rain: grasshoppers
bounce off through the weeds like coins.
A breeze in the blaze of aspens;
sun hums in the frozen sweep of spruce.

You are tired,
like the dry earth.
But unlike it
you know too much.
For still, that is
earth's definition:
whatever it knows,
that is enough.

And because it is fall,
darkness will shadow the northwest;
and because it is late in this century,
darkness will be in the air you breathe.
And because you are human, darkness
has come from your hand,
your mouth,
and it thickens around your heart
like fat around a liver: you will never
know enough.

For you are alive:

here, sitting in the dirt,
the clumps of shorn alfalfa,
the crack in the dust,
hay down your collar, a wasp, the aspens
luminous, the luminous sky
big as an outflung arm.

　　　　　　　For this is the world:
even you, with your hands, and your language,
and your fat black heart.

And the light,
the light shines on it.

V

And I misread the coda, too:
thought you thought
you'd heard some angel
clattering on the stairs.

But no.
The floundering, the rage, fistfuls
of wrong-shaped emptiness: you knew
as well as anyone.
God comes from the darkness—
if he comes—
like pain from a wound,
frost from concrete,
the next step.

Which is not to say
there is no joy—only that
it's never a reward.
That's all you meant:
the sweetest truth, or the most terrible,
can fly up, just like that, be lost
like dust in sunlight.

Contributors

JEANETTE ARMSTRONG is an Okanagan Indian, born and raised on the Penticton Indian Reserve in British Columbia. Her publications include *Break Tracks* and *Slash*. She lives in the Okanagan, where she is currently director of the En'owkin Centre, an Indigenous cultural, educational, ecological and creative arts post-secondary institution.

MARGARET ATWOOD was born in Ottawa, Ontario. She has published ten novels including *The Handmaid's Tale*, *Alias Grace* and *Oryx and Crake*. Her many poetry collections include *The Circle Game*, *The Journals of Susanna Moodie*, *Procedures for Underground*, *Murder in the Dark*, and *Morning in the Burned House*. She lives in Toronto.

KEN BABSTOCK was born in Burin, Newfoundland, and grew up in the Ottawa Valley. His books include *Mean* and *Days into Flatspin*. He is currently serving as Poetry Editor at Anansi Press, and reviews regularly for *The Globe and Mail*. He lives in Toronto.

CHRISTIAN BÖK was born in Toronto. His books include *Crystallography*, *Eunoia*, and *Pataphysics: The Poetics of an Imaginary Science*. He is Assistant Professor of English at the University of Calgary.

GEORGE BOWERING was born in Summerland, British Columbia. His books of poetry include *Kerrisdale Elegies*, *His Life*, and *Changing on the Fly*. He was Canada's first Poet Laureate and is a professor emeritus at Simon Fraser University. He lives in Vancouver.

DIONNE BRAND was born in Trinidad. Her books include the poetry collections *No Language is Neutral*, *Land to Light On*, and *Thirsty*, and the novel *Another Place, Not Here*. Brand lives north of Toronto. She has been writer-in-residence at the University of Guelph.

NICOLE BROSSARD was born in Montréal, Québec, where she currently lives and writes. Selected publications include *Mauve Desert*, *Picture Theory*, *Installations*, *The Blue Books*, and *Museum of Bone and Water*.

DIANA FITZGERALD BRYDEN was born in London, England. Her publications include *Learning Russian* and *Clinic Day*. She works as a writer in Toronto.

ANNE CARSON lives in Canada. Her publications include *Short Talks, Autobiography of Red, The Beauty of the Husband, Men in the Off Hours* and *If Not, Winter: Fragments of Sappho.*

GEORGE ELLIOTT CLARKE was born in Windsor, Nova Scotia. Selected publications include, *Blue, Whylah Falls, Beatrice Chancey, Odysseys Home: Mapping African-Canadian Literature,* and *Eyeing the North Star: Directions in African-Canadian Literature.* He lives in Toronto where he is professor of English Literature at the University of Toronto.

LORNA CROZIER was born in Swift Current, Saskatchewan. Publications include *What the Living Won't Let Go,* A *Saving Grace, Everything Arrives at the Light,* and *Inventing the Hawk.* She teaches in the Creative Writing Department at the University of Victoria.

MARY DALTON was born in Lake View, Conception Bay, Newfoundland. Her book of poems, *Merrybegot,* was published in 2004. Dalton lives in St. John's and teaches in the Department of English at Memorial University

JOE DENHAM was born in Perth, Ontario. *Flux* was published in 2003. Denham is a fisherman who lives on Lasqueti Island in British Columbia.

CHRISTOPHER DEWDNEY was born in London, Ontario. Publications include *The Natural History, Demon Pond, Radiant Inventory,* and *Signal Fires.* He currently lives in Toronto and teaches in Environmental Studies at York University.

SUSAN GOYETTE was born in Sherbrooke, Quebec. Her publications include *True Names of Birds, Undone,* and a novel *Lures.* She is on the faculty at the Sage Hill School and lives in Halifax.

LYDIA KWA was born in Singapore and has lived in Canada since 1980. Her publications include *The Colours of Heroines,* a collection of poems, and *This Place Called Absence,* a novel. Kwa is a clinical psychologist in private practice in Vancouver.

SONNET L'ABBÉ was born in Toronto. Her first collection of poems, *A Strange Relief* was published in 2001. She is a freelance writer and currently works in News Services at the University of Toronto. She lives just west of Toronto's Little Italy.

DENNIS LEE was born in Toronto. His books of poetry include the *Civil*

Elegies and Other Poems; Riffs; and *Un;* and, for children, *Alligator Pie, Nicholas Knock and Other People,* and *Garbage Delight.* Formerly the primary lyricist for the television program *Fraggle Rock,* he lives in Toronto where he is the city's poet laureate.

TIM LILBURN was born in Regina, Saskatchewan. His publications include *Names of God, Moosewood Sandhills,* and *Kill-site.* He teaches at the University of Victoria.

DAPHNE MARLATT was born in Melbourne, Australia. Selected publications include *Seven Glass Bowls, This Tremor Love Is, Steveston, Readings from the Labyrinth, Taken,* and *Ana Historic.* She lives in Vancouver and is writer-in-residence at Simon Fraser University.

DON McKAY was born in Owen Sound, Ontario. Publications include *Moccasins on Concrete: Poems, Air Occupies Space, Long Sault, Lependu, Birding, or Desire, Night Field: Poems, Apparatus, Another Gravity, Vis à Vis: Fieldnotes on Poetry and Wilderness,* and *Camber: Selected Poems.* McKay is on faculty at Sage Hill and Banff Center for the Arts, and lives in in Victoria, British Columbia.

ERIN MOURÉ / EIRIN MOURE was born in Calgary, Alberta. Her books include *O Cidadán, Search Procedures, The Green Word: Selected Poems 1973–1992,* and *Furious,* as well as translations from the French and Portuguese. She has been Writer-in-Residence at the University of New Brunswick, and lives in Montréal, Quebec, where she works as a translator.

bp NICHOL was born in Vancouver, British Columbia. Publications include *The Martyrology Books 1–7, The Captain Poetry Poems, Konfessions of an Elizabethan fan dancer, Love: A book of remembrances,* and *Zygal.* Nichol died in 1988, just before his 44th birthday.

MICHAEL ONDAATJE was born in Sri Lanka and has lived in Canada since 1963. His prose publications include the novels *The Conversations: Walter Murch and the Art of Editing Film, Anil's Ghost, The English Patient, In the Skin of a Lion, Coming Through Slaughter, The Collected Works of Billy the Kid;* and his memoir, *Running in the Family.* His collections of poetry include *Secular Love, The Cinnamon Peeler* and *Handwriting.* He lives in Toronto.

ANNE SIMPSON was born in Toronto. Her publications include two books of poetry, *Light Falls Through You* and *Loop,* and a novel, *Canterbury Beach.* Simpson works at St. Francis Xavier University, in Antigonish, Nova Scotia, where she resides.

KAREN SOLIE was born in Moose Jaw, Saskatchewan. She is the author of *Short Haul Engine* and *Modern and Normal.* She currently resides in Edmonton, where she is writer-in-residence at the University of Alberta.

TODD SWIFT was born in Montreal, Quebec. He is the author three poetry collections, *Budavox, Café Alibi,* and *Rue de Regard;* and the editor of five anthologies. He is the poetry editor of the online magazine *nthposition* and lives in London's West End.

FRED WAH was born in Swift Current, Saskatchewan. He is the author of *Diamond Grill, Alley Alley Home Free, Music at the Heart of Thinking, Waiting For Saskatchewan, Breathin' My Name With a Sigh,* and *Pictograms from the Interior of B.C.* He recently retired from the University of Calgary, and lives in Vancouver.

JAN ZWICKY was born in Alberta, Canada. Selected publications include *Songs for Relinquishing the Earth, Robinson's Crossing, Lyric Philosophy, Wisdom & Metaphor,* and *37 Small Songs and 13 Silences.* She is a professor at the University of Victoria, where she resides.

Acknowledgments

Thanks to the following copyrights holders for permission to reprint the poems included in *Open Field*:

"Winds", "Green", and "Blood" from *Breath Tracks* by Jeanette Armstrong, Theytus Books. Copyright © 1990 Jeanette Armstrong. Used by permission of Theytus Books and the author.

"The Loneliness of the Military Historian", "The Moment" taken from *Morning in the Burned House* by Margaret Atwood. Used by permission of McClelland & Stewart Ltd., *The Canadian Publishers*. "Strawberries", and "Autobiography" taken from *Murder in the Dark* by Margaret Atwood. Used by permission of McClelland & Stewart Ltd., *The Canadian Publishers*.

"First Lesson In Unpopular Mechanics" and "What We Didn't Tell The Medic" from *Mean* by Ken Babstock, House of Anansi Press. Used by permission. "Palindrome" and "Pragmatist" included as per agreement with the author.

Excerpts from "Chapter A for Hans Arp", "Chapter E for René Crevel", "Chapter I for Dick Higgins", "Chapter O for Yoko Ono", and "Chapter U for Zhu Yu" from *EUNOIA* by Christian Bök, Coach House Books, 2001. Reprinted with the permission of the author.

"Elegy One" from *Kerrisdale Elegies* by George Bowering, Coach House Press, 1984. Reprinted with the permission of the author.

Excerpts from "Every Chapter Of The World" from *Land to Light On* by Dionne Brand. Reprinted by permission of McClelland & Stewart, *The Canadian Publishers*.

"Typhoon Thrum" from *Museum of Bone and Water* by Nicole Brossard. Copyright 1999 Éditions du Noroît and Cadex Éditions. English translation copyright 2003 House of Anansi Press. Reprinted with the permission of House of Anansi Press, Toronto.

"Sleepers Awake", "Always, Not Always", "Age And The Secretary", "Clinic Day", "Fertility Test" from *Clinic Day* by Diana Fitzgerald Bryden, Brick Books 2004. Reprinted by permission of Brick Books.

"Short Talk On Gertrude Stein About 9:30", "Short Talk On Trout", "Short Talk On Walking Backwards", "Short Talk On Reading", "Short Talk On The Youth at Night", "Short Talk On Orchids", "Short Talk On The Truth To Be Had From Dreams", "Short Talk On The Sensation Of Aeroplane Take off", first appeared in SHORT TALKS, by Anne Carson, published by Brick Books, 1992. Subsequently published in PLAINWATER, Knopf, 1995. Copyright © by Anne Carson. Reprinted by permission of Anne Carson.

"The Student's Tale", "Blank Sonnet", "The Wisdom Of Shelley", "Prelude", "Monologue For Selah Bringing Spring To Whylah Falls", "To Selah", "Quilt", and